When Mother is a Prefix

WHEN MOTHER IS A PREFIX

New Directions in Youth Correction

by
Nelson Henry

Behavioral Publications   New York
1972

Library of Congress Catalog Card Number   70-184154
Standard Book Number 87705-075-9
Copyright © 1972 by Behavioral Publications

BEHAVIORAL PUBLICATIONS,
2852 Broadway—Morningside Heights,
New York, New York 10025

Printed in the United States of America

CONTENTS

Foreword

With Affection
to
Harriet, Pamela, Suzanne, and Todd,
and with hope for a better future,
to caged boys everywhere.

FOREWORD

This book is for counselors, the men who labor in the unfruitful vineyards of youth correction, and for the curious, who may have wondered what goes on behind the gray walls and wire-meshed windows of our youth houses.

Also it is for supervisors and administrators because I, a former counselor, have much to say to them, but am not always able to do it directly. Often it is about them, and when what is said seems malevolent, it is only in the sense that a man who describes a ruined picnic must discuss the rain or the ants.

But mostly I discuss what goes on and what should go on between the boys and their leaders, the counselors. It is hoped that through the experiences, case histories and proposals described herein, our counselors and their boys will be able to grow into a higher relationship level.

The technique, insofar as there is a technique, is called the Relations Method. It is simply a more sensitive and more practical look at the man-boy relationship and tells how the "growth drive," a tendency possessed by all children, can be mobilized for their improvement.

I offer no gimmicks, no magic potions and no sociological moon shots. All the triumphs in youth work that I have witnessed and have enjoyed have been won through persistent effort and sincere involvement on the part of the counselor. For, whatever the name is which applies to an approach and however "new" the method, be assured that determination and sincerity are two counselor qualities that will never be out of style. I simply propose a way to get more mileage out of them. And with the distance you and your boys have to travel to get to that place called "rehabilitation," a better, pollution-free fuel is needed to replace the old smog-makers that our institutions have been burning.

Book I
The Counselor and The Group

1. ORIENTATION

TO THE COUNSELOR:

I'm going to ask you to do something fantastic. I'm going to ask you to forget your lousy pay, your aching back, your sleepwalking administrators, and those long hours, and to do something that is almost never done where you work. Before we begin, I should warn you that if we are successful in what I am about to propose, it will make no new friends for you, no extra pay, no notices in the newspapers, and no invitations to appear on anyone's TV talk show. I'm going to ask you actually to help the boys housed in your detention home or industrial school or youth house or wherever bars and steel screens separate boys from society.

No, I'm not some armchair humanitarian or "revolutionary," flapping his coattails in the present gales of social protest, oozing little puffs of advice between cocktails. The places where I have worked were just like the one where you are now laboring, and my head was just as low in the bureaucratic pecking order as yours, that is, at the bottom. But over the years I have watched two things happen in America that, like the counterweights on a seesaw, escalate each other to ever new heights of despair. They are the rapidly rising juvenile and adult crime rates and the worsening conditions within the places where boys who get into trouble or are abandoned are supposed to be helped.

I have been employed in detention homes, diagnostic centers, children's homes, and schoolrooms over the past seventeen years in three large, northern, industrial cities and have seen the pattern develop with an outcome as predictable as the plot of yesterday's soap opera. When the population grows and the facilities for the care of wayward youngsters don't, when the budgetary allotment for the hiring of personnel is kept at the 1955 level with a 1971 population in the boys' homes, and when the public clamor for more arrests of juvenile offenders is matched in ferocity only by the political reluctance to spend more money for rehabilitation, a pincers closes in and the boys are caught in the middle. And they feel it. They feel it in the sweltering, jampacked cubicles where they must sleep, in the pigpen dormitories where they must while away the weeks and months waiting for trial or deliverance to "industrial schools." Together with their overburdened counselors, they feel it in classrooms that operate on half-day schedules for lack of teachers and overabundance of inmates, in instructorless shop classes and abandoned remedial education programs.

Now there is little that you and I can do about any of that. The present mood of America is not for the salvation of erring souls but for their punishment, and once having punished them, to sweep the debris under the rug of "urban renewal" and "preventive detention" camps. In other words, so far as a large segment of American opinion is concerned, the boys in your care can go to hell, so long as they do so quietly and out of camera range, behind the billboards of chamber-of-commerce propaganda. That, we shall not overcome.

The irony—and whatever hope—in the present dilemma is that you—we—are potentially quite powerful, insofar as the quality of domestic life that urban America experiences over the next several years depends to a great extent on what we do now, or fail to do. How so? For eight hours each day, the tens of thousands of boys who in a year's time are housed in the detention homes and youth centers around the country are in our laps. America has said, "Keep 'em quiet, controlled, and *there,*" stamped them "no deposit-no return," and hustled off to watch the Dow-Jones scoreboard.

To put it more positively, for eight hours each day we have a captive audience of the boys who, if their lives are not somehow reconstructed, will form the nucleus of the next generation of the unemployed, the welfare-dependent, the absentee fathers, the criminals and addicts. The FBI Uniform Crime Report of 1967 states that 70 per cent of those arrested as juveniles will be rearrested as adults. In other words, if we will but take it, we counselors and schoolteachers have the last best shot at effecting an improvement in those shattered lives, remolding attitudes along positive lines. And that is what this book is all about. I have outlined a method that over the years has proved effective in bringing about this desired change in those lads who have not been so bruised that they are unreceptive to new ideas. It is referred to as the Relations Method. Case histories are included throughout to illustrate the successes, disappointments, and triumphs that any counselor, good or untalented, might experience while developing and sharpening his skill. It is my hope that a prior, vicarious acquaintance with these possibilities will shorten the distance between your wanting to be a good counselor and becoming one.

Now in your present function as youth custodian, your contact with the boys has been officially reduced to the lowest human denominator, which is merely their clothing and feeding. What seems to escape the awareness of those officials who have determined this relationship is that every boy whom we, through neglect or stupidity, fail to guide toward hope represents a loss to a society that can't afford to lose anyone. The potential damage to ourselves is almost unimaginable. Think, for example, of the possible impact on world history of a truly rehabilitated Lee Harvey Oswald, who spent part of his early years in a New York children's home; or the importance to the Cutter family of Kansas of a reformed Perry Smith, who was one of their murderers and who was also a children's home resident.

A secondary purpose in writing this book is to try to make the operators of these rickety systems more self-conscious, to redirect the consistent mismanagement of the lives of boys who have, through some misfortune, been assigned to their care. You, as counselors, are part of these operations and, morose as the present situation is, herein lies your opportunity to count for something worthwhile in those lives. For this reason I have elected to make my pitch for reform to those at the middle and bottom of the bureaucratic pyramid and to suggest ways in which you can wage this needed revolution from below—which amounts really to how to become good counselors in spite of a system that rewards you for being poor ones.

How important is it that you make the effort? One way to answer this is to look at the monetary cost of failure. Crime costs the United States over thirty-two billion dollars per year. That breaks down to one hundred sixty dollars per year for every man, woman, and child; the money goes for the maintenance of prisons, jails, detention homes, bigger police forces and arsenals, property lost and damaged, and so on. That's merely the cost in money. More grievous is the cost in lives, not just of the criminals slain or of their victims, but in the lives of those jailed boys whose potential for good contributions to a foundering society is lost forever through just the kind of detention-home bungling of which you may be a part.

This book is not an expose. For anyone whose stomach is strong enough, the libraries and newspapers are full of disclosures of the backwardness of our "rehabilitation centers." And I have given up hope that a slumbering public can be roused to wreak the kind of reform attack this situation cries out for. The one big chance the boys have left lies with those "involved" administrators who labor in the middle tiers of policy formulation and with the counselors, cottage parents, youth leaders, and schoolteachers who are with the boys hour by hour, day by day. They can, if they will, seize the time spent with their charges to make certain that policy serves them and not the reverse.

You are not going to save all of them; you may not even get through to most. But the thing to keep in mind is that every boy in whom you manage to reinstill hope and a desire for self-improvement is one more hedge against tomorrow's crime statistics, one more brick in the dike against tomorrow's tragedy.

We haven't much time left. A casual reading of our daily newspapers reminds us, perhaps warns us, that a new and different America of undefined character is in the offing. We have just left a decade when social programs for righting old social wrongs held high esteem with federal planners, when innovative planning was prominent in political rhetoric if not in official action, a decade that may have represented the watershed of governmental concern with the problems of the poor, the backward, the antisocial acting-outers. The programs that were started, such as storefront youth centers, child-care centers, police athletic leagues, Head Start, and others, just did not (perhaps could not) do the job. While it may be argued that there were political, economic, and bureaucratic reasons for their failure, the future America thundering upon us may be even less tolerant, less understanding and, yes, less guilt-ridden than we are at present. Let us be honest and admit that those of us who entreated the American conscience to redeem her disadvantaged black and misunderstood white young got a hell of a lot of mileage out of that guilt. Free lunch programs, free medical care, remedial reading programs, Manpower Training, and other conscience-easing tokens(?) would not have stood the chance of a fart in a whirlwind of implementation had it not been for the pressure of guilt and, it must be admitted, the threat of violence. For some mystical reason that needs psychological investigation, American officialdom is more responsive to Molotov cocktails than to reasoned entreaty.

All rivers go somewhere; the flood of conscience-inspired social reforms has about dried up. The spring of 1971 found massive state and federal budgetary cutbacks in public services that would have been most helpful to the communities from which your boys come. If I can trust the impression that boredom flickered in the eyes of those peace demonstrators—the harbingers of our coming "greener" America—when domestic reform issues were raised at their rallies, it would seem that the future will demand more rather than less from our perennial losers. And when there is no official repression, no institutionalized racism, no unreconstructed presidents, and no undesegregated schools and industries, at whose door will we lay the blame for the boys within these pages? For they or their descendants will still be with us. National guilt will be a dead nag then, never again to be flayed into action by social hustlers. The "greener" Americans, having labored for this future of peace and freedom, having campaigned for a reordering of priorities, will feel that they have paid their dues.

A foretaste of the hardening of the humanitarian spirit is shown by the Greenwich Villagers' demand that the New York police understand less and do more to sweep the streets of addicts and pushers. Never mind what happens to them, just get them out of our neighborhood. This occurred coincidentally with the threatened closing of many of New York City's narcotic rehabilitation centers in a massive economy drive. After all, addicts don't vote. The white parents of the northeast Bronx who read of dope epidemics in their newly integrated schools and whose children come home complaining of threats and assaults mutter bitterly, "Never again." And one can be doubly assured of the Spartan expectations of this coming America when one considers that it is now black citizens, along with a great many whites, who clamor for tougher law-enforcement measures—including preventive detention—to stem the escalating burden of street muggings and gang assaults in their communities. This was notably true in Harlem.

So the clock is ticking faster for our unrehabilitated boys. There is little time left. It is my hope that in this last hour before midnight, the suggestions made in the pages following will enable some child-care workers and counselors of delinquent boys to improve some lad's attitude, to (as the saying goes) "get him together," before his future dissolves into a rotten pumpkin, scurrying rats, and a long night of despair.

No, the Relations Method is not magical. Sometimes it fails, and for the sake of candor I have included some of these setbacks among my case histories. But it is far better than most of the techniques that I have seen employed in the youth centers I have labored in, and I believe it best prepares the antisocial youngster to face whatever it is that he must face.

2. THE PLANT

Before we get into the how's and what-to-do-when's of relations counseling, it might be well for you as a guy who wants to do a good job to know exactly what you may be up against. The main obstacle preventing you from helping a youngster, say, a veteran street fighter or purse snatcher or chronic truant, to change his self-destructive and outwardly aggressive attitude is not the viciousness of the boy, not his low academic achievement, not the fact that he has been that way for years and the habit is too strong to break, not necessarily the presence of a neurosis, though this may at times contribute, and not the fact that for twelve or fourteen years he has lived in a home where there was implied condonement of his type of behavior—although it would be foolish to deny that some or all of these factors may play a part. Never have I seen all of them at work in one boy; even so, one of these impairments is plenty. However, the big roadblock that I have had to hurdle in most of the places where I have worked is what might rightly be called Institutional Somnambulism, that is, administrative sleepwalking.

When a man sleepwalks, he may stub his toe, tumble down a staircase, bump into a clothes rack, walk out into midnight traffic, or do any of a dozen things that for the most part are injurious only to himself. But when an institution dazedly stumbles through a day-by-day routine, particularly one charged with the responsibility for hundreds of already damaged lives, glued hypnotically to traditional pathways of child mismanagement that lead like the legendary elephant walk to a graveyard of failure and missed opportunities, it is a lapse of foresight that is horrendous in magnitude and consequences. To put it in plainer language, you're going to have to breach the faith, baby. You're going to have to elevate your relationship to the boys above the baby-sitting level of feeding them and putting them to bed, to one more human, more intimate, and more meaningful. That's not easy. The yearly turnover in good counselors is about equal to that of Macy's revolving door. No one likes to be stepped on by an elephant.

A true elephant story: I once asked a supervisor why a certain fifteen-year-old boy who had run away from his home in South Carolina and was brought by the police to our center could not be shortly enrolled in the center school. Like many black refugees from the South, he was functionally illiterate; once he got past reading and writing his own name he was through. However, another counselor and I soon discerned that he was extremely bright and, better yet, eager to learn by attending our school. I was told that state law dictated that out-of-state runaways could not be enrolled, no matter what. And furthermore, the story went on, he would soon be sent back home, so a short-term enrollment wouldn't do him that much good anyway. So Abraham, as he was called, languished in the dormitory while the other young-sters trooped out to our underattended classrooms. He spent the days looking at comic books, playing records, getting into an occasional fight and otherwise wasting his time. My chagrin increased when weeks passed and he still wasn't sent home—or enrolled in school. When he finally left us, still illiterate, he had been there long enough to have made a good start at some of the basic educational skills, had he been allowed to. Incidentally, "soon" in administrative jargon means between now and the millennium. To this day I have a hard time getting it through my thick skull that the governor or the state superintendent of education or the mayor would have given a damn if this kid had been allowed to attend our school. The irony of it was that the dorms were full of boys who quite literally had to be dragged up to the schoolrooms and then virtually chained to their desks. But Abe wanted to go and couldn't. Whatever the broader implications of this episode, it brings us around to a good point of departure for our philosophy of relations counseling, and that is, every boy is important, particularly an eager beaver like Abe. We cannot afford to lose a single prospect, but I am afraid we flubbed that one.

The places where the city or state governments house delinquent and abandoned boys go by different names and claim for themselves a variety of functions. Regardless of the stated distinctions, some of them artificial, they all have three things in common: a small staff of counselors whose practical task is to see that the boys don't tear the plant or each other apart; large numbers of boys who have long ago outgrown the rated capacity of the plant; and administrators. From the standpoint of what is supposed to go on inside, these places may be subdivided into three broad categories: detention homes, diagnostic centers, and children's shelters.

A detention home is a building or group of buildings where boys who have run afoul of the law are kept until their cases are brought up for trial in municipal or county court. One very useful function of the detention home is that it saves the youngster from confinement in the city or county jail, where his cellmates might be hardened criminals or perverts. The doors of the detention home are, of course, locked. His period of confinement may range from two weeks to almost a year, depending on the court calendar and on whether the boy's family can get a decent lawyer.

A diagnostic center is theoretically a place where socially maladjusted boys are sent by court order for observation, evaluation, and diagnosis. Here you will find the greatest concentration of clinical psychologists, social workers and psychiatrists. On paper the setup looks great. I remember watching a TV program that dealt with juvenile problems, in which the judge announced to a first offender that he was sending him to the state facility in the capital, where he could be diagnosed, treated, and returned to society a better boy. The dignity, the hauteur with which the jurist intoned the benediction, "state diagnostic center," conveyed, as I am sure it was meant to, the impression that the center was some wondrous place where the bureaucratic gears

meshed with the boy's broken-down machinery to roll
out a bright new personality stamped "good" or
"socialized" or something like that. I collapsed laughing,
because at that time I was working there and the only
thing that was "done" was the staff in the sense that we
were done *in* by overcrowding, low morale, staff
shortages, poor supply schedules, administrative hang-
ups, the whole bit.

The third category, perhaps the broadest, is that of the
children's shelter. Here we might also include the honor
camps and halfway houses, where boys who are not
quite ready to be returned to their communities are sent
for a final "rounding off" process. Unlike the first two
categories, the doors of the children's shelters are not
locked and, perhaps surprisingly, the unlocked door is a
powerful aid in the hand of the counselor.

There are a number of pathways along which a boy
might wind his way to such a haven. One is through
court remand: a judge decides that the parents of a youth
are negligent, contributory to his delinquency or abusive
of him, and sends him there. Or it may be a simple case
of a runaway child for whom temporary quarters are
needed. Or a deserted mother is just too poor to keep him.
I have seen entire newly immigrated Latin families
unloaded on a children's shelter on this basis. The open-
door policy dictates that any child who needs temporary
shelter gets it. Whatever the nature of the institution in
which you work, the boys there all need one thing that
life outside failed to provide, the motivation for growth
toward self-fulfillment; and your tremendous importance
rests in the fact that if they don't get it from you, the
chances of their getting it at all are slim indeed.

I have purposely omitted boarding schools, boys'
ranches, and parochial homes from our survey for two
reasons. One is that they are privately funded and can
therefore exercise selectivity in their admissions. The
second is that the effective distance between the ad-
ministrator's office and the boys' rooms is much shorter
than in public facilities. This does not mean that many
of the problems inherent in public institutional care do
not also afflict them, but the fact that they are private

confers on them a wider range of options in solving them. For instance, turning out a recalcitrant youngster is one of them. Those of us in public homes must keep them and somehow work out their and our salvation.

3. ORIGINS

There are many things that could be said about the origin of our refugees but which must be omitted, because to discuss them would expand this writing beyond its stated purpose. In fact, most of these factors are quite well known. I could discuss, for example the implication of racially exclusionary hiring practices in construction companies, apprenticeship programs, and the notoriously racist construction unions in the creation of chronic unemployment among blacks and Puerto Ricans and their consequent relegation to low-paying service jobs. Some families are into their third generation on public assistance. They form part of a growing subculture in which the "normal" income expectancy is reliance on public subsidy. A New York social worker reported her bemusement when during a home visit she noticed her client's children playing a game generally unknown to children outside this subculture. The game is "welfare." They cheerfully assumed the roles of the needy mother trying to wheedle more money out of "that white caseworker," the caseworker, the man picking up "numbers" money, and so on. Among them, cops and robbers, house, and tag were all passe.

I could mention the apparent paralysis of leadership and purpose of successive presidential administrations in the solution of the rampant growth of unemployment, poor housing, and the need for welfare assistance among thirty million citizens. Robber-baron landlords, loan sharks, narcotics importers, indifferent or incompetent school officials could all be discussed *ad nauseum* for their contributions to the origins of our boys. I suspect, however, that nothing short of a popular (hopefully peaceful) revolution can change this, in which a majority of Americans, finally disgusted and sickened by the diet

13

of lies and betrayals fed them by those who control our political destinies and national economic style, would act to bring forth a new, "greener" era. Unfortunately, I don't know how to bring that day closer. What I do have to offer are some modest suggestions on what to do for the by-products of these social atrocities until the revolution comes.

4. THE THEORETICAL BASIS OF RELATIONS COUNSELING

Before we sail out onto the uncharted waters of relations counseling, let me state again in somewhat more stark language the reasons why this trip is necessary. We counselors, group leaders, child-care workers, supervisors, et al., are generally doing one lousy job of helping our youngsters, and the one success that I can credit us with is our ability to cop all kinds of pleas why we aren't doing better. Next to Washington bureaucrats, we are the world's best excuse finders. I have heard every alibi imaginable, from the boys' "dumbness" to slippage of the Polar Ice Cap, cited as reasons for our not doing what we are, in fact, able to do. This is not a super-righteous put-down from some dewy-eyes idealist. In some of my weaker moments of years past, I too was part of the chorus of poor-mouthers whose "hands were tied." In fact, this book lays the burden of rehabilitative failures on someone other than ourselves: administrators and government apathy, where indeed it belongs. But one difference in my present attitude is that I know it does no good to flail away at these twin blocks of granite from our present position, any more than throwing marshmallows at a Sherman tank will knock it over. The important point I want to put across here is that it is possible through the proposals made herein to promote the rehabilitative process in spite of the administrative elephants blocking the path. So, without further ado, let us cast off while the tide is in. I can see storm clouds gathering inland with gale winds of public opinion howling "The hell with 'em—throw away the key!" We would hate for our boys to be caught with their anchors down.

The counselor who is interested in attitudinal reform among his boys must remember that he is dealing not only with bodies and names and records of listed offenses, but that each youngster represents a hard-to-define something called *mind*. And it is toward this concept of him that relations counseling bends its efforts. Let me talk about it in as simple terms as such a complex function will allow.

Think of the mind of a youngster as an erector set. It is a rather curious tool, one that was laid on him *in part* by his parents at the moment of conception. I say "in part" because for some reason just the nuts and bolts and a few cables belonging to it are present at birth; it is not a completely assembled ability. There are parts of it that are missing, vital parts that can only be acquired from outside the infant and growing child. Now, in the baby of normal health, normal physical make-up, and adequate nutrition, this unassembled erector set begins doing something wonderful the moment the doctor delivers its possessor. It begins to gather or collect those vital parts without which it cannot grow, without which it must remain throughout life an unassembled, nonfunctioning collection of nuts and bolts and limp cables.

What are these parts? Psychologists refer to them as external stimuli. Let us stay down-to-earth and call them simply the bits and pieces of the world as we know it and experience it. Among them are touch and the pressure of hands on the baby's skin, sounds and noises and his mother's voice, warmths and coolnesses and drynesses and moistures, sensations of falling or uplift and of what must be the powerful stimulation of moist touch around his mouth. These are all solid, tangible things and the erector set works marvelously with them. For example, the moist touch at his lips followed soon afterward by the pleasing fullness in his gut locks a bolt or pulley into place; or the sound of footsteps followed soon afterward by warm squeezing gets the crane moving more efficiently, the cables sliding more smoothly. Piece by piece, with marvelous speed, the parts and impressions from the outside are manipulated and assembled to make up a "total view" (mind view) of the infant's environment.

And of course the more of these erector parts that are thrown or stimulated into service, the better able is baby's mind to organize the fantastically larger array of pieces it will be confronted with as the child grows older.

A funny thing about this erector set. At times it doesn't seem to be too careful about the outside pieces that it chooses to make a part of itself. While it is true that many of the things it incorporates are what we older folk would call "good," such as avoiding matches after being burned once or learning to pee in the potty rather than on the rug, it is just as quick to add things we would label "bad." Now, if the youngster's mother is watchful and energetic, she usually tries to help out in this selection process, giving little rewards for choices that are "good" and little penalties for "bad" ones. And the erector set, being a truly marvelous machine, generally follows this guidance (with lapses—minor breakdowns—now and then, called tantrums or misbehavior). All the while, the set is getting bigger, that is, controlling more and more of the choice making and more and more of the child's environment. By age five, one would swear that mind had outstripped the physical growth of the youngster, so frenzied are its grabs for environmental knickknacks, so tightly does it lock them into place (known to psychologists as learning and memory development). In fact, our erector set has now reached such a level of complexity of functions that we can no longer encompass all of them, even using a mechanical model, for it is now equipped with hundreds of rods and beams and cables performing thousands of different tasks that are, we suspect, somehow related. Indeed, the more we watch people in action, the more convinced we become that all mind's motives and moves boil down to a few basic jobs. We will discuss two of them, for they are the key to how we may help our boys.

From the time, eons ago, when the first amphibian creature crawled out of the sea and blinked in the unfamiliar brightness of the sun, each living being has had to achieve two absolutely essential tasks, or it vanished forever from the earth. They were (and are): preservation of the self and reproduction of one's kind. The ways in which we achieve these goals, the styles and techniques that are employed are as varied as there are numbers of living things in existence. Mind, far from being the human attribute that elevates man above the salamander, actually links him to his unrevered past because mind, for all its complexity, demands that he shall do what the sea urchin and the clam and the salamander do. Never mind the flourishes and the side shows, the fantastic elaborateness of the acts that mind enables us to perform; the direction of these drives is to "take care of business," that is, doing the anciently determined job of species survival.

Now the erector set, going back to our mechanical model, possessed by man is in many ways not as efficient as those of the salamander and the robin and the earthworm. Theirs have built-in selectors that eliminate the need for someone to help in the selection of "good" and the avoidance of "bad" pieces from the environment. Nest-building, sand-burrowing and swimming don't have to be demonstrated and taught to these "lower" beings. Nature sets the survival autopilot on "go" at the instant they crawl out of their egg or cyst or whatever they crawl out of, and they are all set. For a number of reasons, which it would not pay us to go into here, the more complex mind is without an autopilot and must achieve its goals through a longer, more diversified route. The most economical way that it can learn to do what the earthworm and robin and salamander are programmed to do is by scooping up and taking in behavior artifacts and pieces from someone who has already learned to do it. That is, by copying a parent model. This model is the first source of the attitudinal and emotional nuts and bolts that the erector set will screw onto itself in its preparation for the battle for self-preservation and reproduction. The drive for the accomplishment of these twin goals is so charged with energy, so demanding of one's emotional and physiological resources that to resist it is to throw the rest of mind's gears out of synchronism. Again, it is our link with our unlamented past. And when anyone seems consciously uninterested in the attainment of either goal (that is, when their emotional gears strip or a couple of cables slip off their pulleys), we consign the possessor of this balky erector set to a repair shop called an insane asylum.

Now what does all this have to do with you and your boys? Just this. Mind, driven by this ancient force with its titanic power, dictates that its possessor, really itself, is going to be "like" someone, that is, make an emotional copy, usually of the parent of the same sex. But what if that parent isn't around? Or what if that parent, while in the home, thwarts the reaching out of mind for him through cruelty or apathy or neglect? Worse yet, what if the copied parent is himself unable to create a winning formula for survival, and mind, having identified with him, merely repeats his failure? These three pitfalls are what have befallen your boys, so that by age seven they begin to replicate their parents' troubles. So universal is the combination of emotional disturbances in parents and children that most family counselors refuse to treat "sick" children unless their parents also agree to come in for conferences.

The duplicating machinery of mind in delinquent children has not been idle, despite the absence or indifference of the parent model. Other models have been chosen and seized upon, like peers (who have the same problems) or an admired antisocial adult in the neighborhood, like the friendly neighborhood pimp. Even when disappointed by parental rejections, abuses and absences, this potent urge remains locked into the erector set's high-powered engine, until by age twelve or sooner the child's coping style, the way he solves life problems, mimics the techniques of his peer or adult model. And if that model is a dope user, a car thief, a purse snatcher, well, then. . . . And this is the attitudinal and emotional background that produced your boys. Given the available blueprints in their environments, it could not be otherwise. Mind could not allow it to be otherwise.

We who would have it different for our youngsters should be grateful to this primordial energy that we share with the salamander and earthworm, for we can use it in the duplication of other, better models, which we will provide them. This is the thrust of the Relations

Method of counseling, the provision of a man among alienated, acting-out boys with whom they, if their erector sets are not already rusted and corroded into immobility and cynicism by bitter experiences, can identify. This is not that tall an order, the finding of such men. I have seen really rotten counselors transform themselves into something worthy of emulation once they saw the light. I was one of them.

5. THE COUNSELOR MODEL

There's a long, long trail awinding, as the song goes, between the admission of a youngster for delinquency and the time when the kind of image-copying that we want to take place will begin. Not only is the trail long, but there must be a well-regulated set of conditions existing before mind, long accustomed to disappointments, can be geared into the dismantling of its anti-social behavior structure and the substitution of a constructive one. The length of this trail and the establishment of these conditions depends to a great extent on the character of the counselor model, you.

Let's say that you are sane—that is, as able as most of us to handle your social and emotional problems—and over twenty-one. You have finished high school and may or may not have completed four years of college. This latter qualification can be of help, but it is no guarantee that you will be better than or even as good as a worker without it, any more than having a box full of hammers will make you necessarily a better carpenter than the guy with only one. It just gives you more leeway in the choice of a tool.

You should also be in pretty good health, not because you may be called upon to outrun or outwrestle anyone, but because the institution you work for and the boys must be able to count on your being there rather consistently. Let's face it; you can't help them or even become significant in their lives if you aren't there most of the time. It may come as a surprise that size is not a factor in the control of your youngsters. An acquaintance of mine, a woman five feet two and one hundred pounds soaking wet, who teaches in Columbus, Ohio, maintains a study hall of over a hundred kids in stark silence, while the same bunch of youngsters have been known to stampede

grown men twice her size. However, I do admit to a bias
in favor of a robust, healthy appearance in the counselor.
Physically, he or she should project vigor, energy, and
dynamism, presumably, if not in fact, the fruit of clean
living. Why? One reason is that it is inevitable that there
will be some identification on the part of the boys with
the man who is paid to lead them. In fact, that's half of
your ball game. It is to be hoped that the object of this
relating is not some bellyaching, pallid shell of a human
being. Another reason is that the counselor often must
convince youngsters who have been living off Cokes and
French fries most of their lives to eat the vitamin-laden
green vegetables, fruits, grain cereals, and milk dished
up by the galley. But if the advocate of proper eating
habits is himself slack-muscled and bleary-eyed, the
obvious question some youngster will ask is, "So what
happened to you?" I know that sometimes the kitchen will
let you down. At one meal the boys were showing a
particular distaste for some salad that looked bright and
tender. I was on their backs about it. Then one kid spoke
up, "You eat it, Mr. Henry. If you do, we will." So I did. It
was the world's worst. The lettuce leaves were as tough
as old inner tubes and as bitter as gall. But I had to eat
every agonizing mouthful. The little devils watched my
expression carefully, and though they ate theirs too, they
knew they had made a point.

For a number of reasons, it is important that you are
not homosexual, at least not so that it shows. What you
do on your own time is, of course, your own business, but
should your boys get wind that you are a trifle "gay," the
extent of ridicule to which you would be subjected, the
suspicions that would be aroused whenever you had to
isolate a boy for a conference, the uneasiness created in
the minds of unliberated supervisors, to say nothing of
the blackmail that you would be vulnerable to should you
blow your control, would reduce your effectiveness to
nothing.

Another major qualification is that you, whatever your
race, be relatively free of racism. I say "relatively"
because it has been a long time since I met an American
of any description who didn't believe down deep that God

had bestowed some exclusive genetic benefit on his tribe. Anyway, the boys are particularly sensitive to the faintest suggestion of favoritism or rejection related to color; and besides, whatever the shade of your hide, you are starting your assignment with a handicap. The social atmosphere of America is so poisonous that many delinquent boys regard any adult of different color or culture as *the enemy,* and this situation is given greater dimension and causes greater anxiety when "the enemy" is in command.

Another minimum assumption relating to personality is the possession of a rather high and stubborn optimism, which will prop you up in those first few weeks when you discover that the job is nothing like the personnel officer described to you.

Counselors who were themselves once residents of ghettos, children's homes, or even of jails, may occasionally be the superior of less knowledgeable workers, once they have been fully rehabilitated. Active felons, alcoholics, or drug addicts cannot be considered in this light. As expected, the level of empathy and depth of understanding that they already have gives them a rather long lead over those of us who have to rely on yet-to-be gained experience and books like this one for our spurs.

If the sight of a lot of tough-looking big boys scares you, I don't need to tell you that you're in the wrong business. It does us no good for me to assure you that they actually are a lot less dangerous than they may look. Fear isn't eradicated that easily, and anyway you will soon convey your timidity to them through your actions and style and call forth the very consequences of which you are so fearful. Still, it needs to be said that there is something about being locked up that takes most of the starch out of a street fighter or mugger, because here is concrete (and steel) evidence that the bag he was in was—as least in this case—the wrong one.

2.

You may as well know at the outset of the broad array

of forces, some psychological, some administrative, that make this job far more difficult than it should be. Consider salary. If you're in this work for the money, you're beyond help by this book or any other. Because there isn't any. The average salary of a children's counselor or schoolteacher is three thousand dollars below what the Federal Government deems to be adequate for a moderate level of living for a family of four. I know of few men who support their families solely on what they make in this vocation, so forget it. You're going to have to cut corners, live with your maiden aunt, farm your wife out to work, or sell newspapers after working hours in order to make ends meet. Therefore, the first axiom to follow in getting yourself really ready is to want to do it; to believe that what you are doing is far more important than that anemic paycheck they shove at you. Because it is.

Next, be ready for disillusionment. Expect, for instance, to find yourself responsible for at least twice the number of boys that the personnel officer mentioned and to find them somewhat more damaged (worse in behavior). It isn't that he tried to deceive you; the option of quitting is too easily available. The truth is often that he himself didn't know. One of the more astounding discoveries you will make about the institutional care of children is the chasm of ignorance that exists between the realities of the classroom or dormitory and the flowery theorizing of the administration. It's like a pregnant woman saying—and believing—that she is a virgin.

I am reminded here of a certain character who runs a children's home in a large northeastern city. His favorite boast is that he started this facility some years ago and has run it ever since. This is, in fact, his stock answer to reporters and union representatives who are so crass as to inquire why the training program for new counselors is so inadequate (two weeks in length, often after the person has worked there for six months or more), or why overcrowding persists, or why sanitation in the kitchen and bathrooms compares unfavorably with the alleys of Calcutta, or why little or no use is made of the long periods the children spend there to teach them basic educational skills or improve their manners or to give them *something* they can use when they leave. Of course, the apartment that the city provides for him within the building is not crowded or unsanitary, there is maid service, rent and board is free, and his salary is generous. When the local newspapers occasionally probe his rotten little operation, he manages either to duck out of his office or give them his stock answer: "I started this shelter over twenty years ago and we do the best we can." This apparently absolves him of responsibility for lax employment practices that frequently leave the boys in the care of alcoholic counselors, counselors with homosexual tendencies, and those who defraud the city of hundreds of dollars per year with phony receipts for movies, the zoo or other trips they were supposed to have taken the boys on. When this so-called superintendent is really pinned to the wall by publicity or bad exposure, I have heard him whine, "I'm only a few years from retirement. It would be stupid of me to do anything that would jeopardize my eligibility for pension and other benefits." Thus this meatball has led the home through decades of bad management—worse, no management, for the children and counselors seldom see him. He doesn't visit the dorms. Then again, why should he? His checks arrive on time and the food, since it is free, can't be complained of. Why bother himself with the problems of management? It's a nice little colonial arrangement, and after all, the city won't miss the money.

But let's go on. Imagination or the ability to improvise quickly is probably the most important extra quality you can possess. It can save you when the "book," that is, the manual of instruction handed you by your supervisor, fails you, as it often does (the reality gap again). Let me describe such a situation.

It is opening day at Yankee Stadium; your co-worker has called in sick (at the last minute). For the last four hours, you have had charge of nineteen little refugees all by yourself. The television set, that great counselor seducer, is on the fritz, and there has been a fight every seven minutes. Incidentally, a television breakdown is one of the worst crises you can have. In the last fight you broke up, you took a hard shot to the kidney. Now your instruction manual, which you memorized, talked much about meaningful activity to structure the boys' time and mentioned games as a favored way to do this. But the game room is locked; your supervisor has the only key and he isn't here. Said something about having to meet his mother-in-law at La Guardia. The crowded dormitory looks like no man's land; another fight is brewing in front of the wrecked TV, and in the bathroom a small knot of boys is rather suspiciously forming. Before you can attend to either, a tiny youngster with a lisp pulls your coattail and complains tearfully that Bruno, a little devil about five feet five in all three dimensions, has hit him for "nah-thing at all." And indeed, he has the red blotch on his cheek indicating that someone has laid one on him. You're going to have to think of something fast, kid. That's what I mean by imagination.

Finally, he prepared not to be paid attention to by your supervisor or principal when you bring him suggestions for improving the lives of the boys. There's a faraway, jaded look that creeps into his eyes, a knowing smile, a furtive glance at his wristwatch, all of which tells you that you're rattling the wrong cage. It isn't that they don't care; they do, some of them desperately. But two things occur to them as you reel off the bright new insights of your experience: one is that they have already tried some of them and found them unworkable; and two, they already know just how dead the bureaucratic dead weight is. What all the above means is that when it actually comes down to helping the boys, you are on your own. Like, all by yourself. I can just hear the chorus of protests rising: "Untrue, untrue! Why, in our state every children's home has available the full-time services of blank numbers of social workers, school psychologists, and psychiatric caseworkers. What the hell does Henry mean, 'all by yourself'?"

It's very simple. What Henry means is that even when these institutions have their full complement of professional help, which they seldom do, the net impact of any one of them on a particular boy is next to nothing.

Like, say, Caspar Milquetoast trying to tackle Jimmy Brown.

Here's how it works—or doesn't work. The number of boys assigned to a particular caseworker may be as high as fifty-five. The average length of stay of the residents is some thirty days. He may or may not get around to seeing all of them more than once, and even then the pressure of his caseload may allow only an hour or so with each. He would have to be persuasive indeed—or hypnotic—for one or two sessions to effect any change in the boy's life. The same is even truer of the school psychologist. His task is to administer evaluative tests and to predict proper placement of the youths. Except in especially hard-core cases, his time per youngster is even less than the caseworker's. So it is the counselor or teacher who has the longest unbroken span of time with the refugees, and therefore the counselor or teacher who has the greatest potential for real help. But get this! In most centers, counselors are advised not to use their opportunity to help on a personal basis. You don't have the expertise, they are told, to aid them in a one-to-one relationship. Leave that to the professionals (who, as I have explained, see them from sixty to one hundred twenty minutes during their stay). While I will allow that some counselors are far more in need of help than the boys, to apply the above as a general rule is ridiculous, because the result of it is that the man-boy relationship remains locked in the dungeon of custodial husbandry. You feed 'em and put 'em to bed; smack 'em down when they get out of line. Boys who come into the detention home as bad little mothers leave as much, much worse little mothers. Tomorrow's thugs are being prehardened by today's custodial methods.

What does all this mean? Simply that you, counselor, are his best—and last—shot before the streets claim him again. You are all this little guy has, and if you are not enough, if the things you tell him, the way you act, your human feeling for him are not enough, make no mistake about it, he's through. The purpose of this book is to bridge the gap between your lack of "expertise" and helping him.

A final revealing word about you and this counseling business. While it may be necessary for you to create strong motivation to be a good counselor or teacher, there are rewards that are already built into the system for being a lousy one. Because if you're a lousy counselor, the job is easy. All you need do is sit there in the dorm or classroom with a contemptuous smile on your face and watch the circus swirl around you. Be sure to duck the flying objects (books, shoes, and the like); there's nothing more undignified than a counselor being brained by a moccasin. Keep sharply abreast of the time and when your eight hours are up, split, regardless of whether your relief has arrived. After all, he may have heard about the madness and decided not to come in. And the beauty of it is that you make just as much as a good counselor.

Of the built-in aggravations that are not directly connected with what you were actually hired to do, clerical work is tops. Of course, the keeping and writing of each day's activity and a summary of the "progress" of each boy is extremely important, as is the making out of requisitions for supplies, taking inventory, ordering repair work, and the like. The hooker is that all this separates you for considerable periods of time from your charges. If you're a poor counselor, that is exactly what you want. It gives you one more reason not to bother yourself with the daily circus—you're too busy writing about it, and if you're a slow writer, there go your eight hours. If you're a good counselor, you begin to look covetously at the six secretaries in the principal's or director's office, some of them busy, some of them counting paper clips. You figure they should be working for you, saving you precious time with your record-keeping. And they should be. Only don't saunter into the office and suggest it, or someone is sure to pull your folder and try to discover how a dumb fellow like you ever got himself hired in the first place. And if you do go in, please don't mention my name.

What I've tried to put across in this little exercise is the conviction that the most potent tools you can carry onto your job are a stubborn optimism and the belief that through alertness, concern and a genuine feeling of humanity for them, you can improve their chances of "making it" in spite of their bruising by the streets. What the good counselor must do is make sure that they aren't further bruised by their experience in his center.

6. THE RELATIONS METHOD OF CHILD GUIDANCE

1.

The rest of this book is about one word, a quite short word, but one whose comprehension can determine whether you become a decent counselor or join the army of zombies currently picking up paychecks twice a month. That word is *relations*.

Relations is a two-dimensional term. On the one hand it refers to what goes on between you and the boys; that is, it defines the quality of the human interaction involving you as their counselor and the boys as the objects of your attention. Now, in the ideal sense, this interaction is one with enough flexibility and mutual trust and respect to promote the total growth of the youngster. It encourages those aspects of his personality that had formerly been squelched or gone unrecognized to bloom, to increase, to become useful and enriching. For example, a boy in Hell's Kitchen who reads and writes poetry may feel as out of place as a black at a Klan meeting (unless, of course, it is a lynching). The erector's demand for instant utility, a hallmark of that corner of our society, just won't allow that kind of indulgence. After all, you can't fight the rats away from baby brother's crib with pentameter verse. And yet, such is the resiliency of the human spirit that great artists, poets, musicians, and writers do issue forth from the basements of our cities. Not in great numbers, to be sure, for this kind of nonconformity finds scant encouragement from derisive peers and indifferent schoolteachers and from the exigencies of daily survival.

But in your center, where it is presumed that fighting vermin is in the capable hands of the exterminators and maintenance men (not always the case, incidentally), it can be hoped that a level of understanding between you and this street-fighter-who-would-be-Byron can progress to a point where he might reveal to you his secret, life-long ambition. And let's face it, if he has the tiniest smidgen of writing talent, it puts him light-years ahead of the present purveyors of popular rock numbers and best (sex) sellers. Now, when he thus confides in you, he is not looking for practical help; indeed, until he en-lightened you about it, you may have thought that "blank verse" was the name of a western hero. What he is, in fact, doing is seeking in you some sign of recogni-tion of the uniqueness of him as an individual and of the worth of what he has chosen as a life vocation. Of course, we all know that ninety-nine per cent of each genera-tion's teenagers, your author among them, who declare that they want to compose deathless sonnets fortunately wind up doing something else. Starving in a garret just isn't the "in" thing any more. But as his friend and confidant, it is not your function to show skepticism or to evaluate his chances of "making it" by versifying (he just *could be* another Byron or Eliot); rather, yours is to serve as a willing, encouraging listener to those construc-tive ideas that may someday develop into concrete, natural avenues for the expression of his talent, whatever it is. In other words, you are helping him to nurture the priceless habit of *future* orientation, of imagining himself in better times, in better company, with a better identity.

The other aspect of relations is concerned with the pre-vailing emotional and social tone in your dorm. It answers the question of how your boys are getting along with each other in terms of their sensitivity to one another's feelings, human needs, the level of emotional support they are likely to grant to those depressed, back-ward, or timid souls who seem so much in need of it, the presence or relative absence of bullying (the bane of dormitory peace), of stealing, of overt homosexuality—in fact, of the entire range of the potentialities for social transactions inherent in a situation of confinement. Now the counselor need not feel that because the state of relations can take so many different pathways it is beyond his competence to determine the outcome, because, in fact, the exact opposite is true. Let me pose the manifold possibilities within the term in another (hopefully clearer) way.

2. AL'S PLACE

Think of a department store with three stories. It is located on a wide thoroughfare named Turmoil Alley, a noisy, brawling street with motorbikes roaring up and down the asphalt, drunks lurching in and out of the taverns lining the sidewalk, and mascaraed preteen girls driving sex bargains with middle-aged lechers who pull up to the curb in limousines. You have to walk carefully to avoid stepping on the derelicts sprawled in stuporous clumps along your path and hop over clots of vomit staining the sidewalk. But worst of all are the junkies begging you for "some change to get downtown to a job," conning you for money, threatening you with their eyes for money, intimidating you, evoking your guilt with their wasted, empty faces and general wretchedness.

You walk in through a revolving door to the ground floor where a guide picks you up. You note how nervous the poor fellow is, all twitches and tics and shifting eyes. The first thing you see is a big red sign saying Anarchy Department; it is crudely lettered and ink drips from the lower edge. When you look around, you are struck by how unnecessary the sign is, for anyone can see the wild disorder. Customers scramble over each other, claw and curse and scream getting up to the counters. Some are knocked down, stepped on and kicked in the mad struggle for merchandise. This may be very good from the owner's standpoint, you surmise, but what a way to shop. Then you are shocked to see that much of the shopware is being lifted in plain view of the store detectives, who are there in great numbers. This doesn't seem to matter; many of them are reading magazines or unconcernedly filing their nails.

The next thing that catches your eye is the merchandise itself, designated by little signs over the counters.

The goods(!) are, to put it mildly, exotic and sold in kits that one can assemble when one gets home. They are easy to identify: Curses and Insults; How to Gouge Out An Eye With A Dull Pencil; Homemade Drugs; Pure Drugs; Knives For The Very Young; Thirteen Dirty Things You Can Do In An Ear Canal With An Icepick; Bruno's Handy Little Assault Kit, and so on. This isn't for you; you can't stand the noise, the riot and, above all, the smell, that of stale sweat. So you follow your guide to the elevator.

A different kind of escort meets you on the second floor. He stands tall, erect, and is very proper indeed. The floor sign proclaims in large, precise letters, Control Department. Floorwalkers are everywhere and are brightly visible in blue, gold-braided uniforms, swinging spiked truncheons. Their eyes sweep the customers constantly, and every so often a detective gooses one of them along with his club.

"Move on, there!"

"You're blocking the aisle; get going!"

"Open up your bag. Do you have a sales slip for everything inside?"

"Get in line; don't shove!" Of course, the customers say nothing, seeming content to shuffle from one counter to the next in quiet, submissive herds.

A second difference is the merchandise, sold in bulkier, unattractive packages: Guaranteed Bowel Control; Muscle Development; Assured Quietness; How To Make Your Bed Though Wanting To Go To The Bathroom; Training Your Bladder; How To Stifle Your Impulses And Love It; Compulsory Good Neighborliness, and the like. All very useful, standard fare. You wonder, though, how anyone can actually enjoy any of it. You look questioningly at your guide, who happens at this instant to be glaring at a customer who accidentally dropped a bottle of shoe polish. The man, who is thoroughly cowed, bends down, wipes up the mess with his sleeve and sidles off. Turning back to you, the guide gives you a gentle but definite shove toward the elevator and says tersely, "Third floor. You may like better what they're selling up there." There is an unmistakable note of condescension in his voice. Before the elevator doors close, you catch a final glimpse of the not-too-unpleasant (by first floor standards) department and see two burly floorwalkers pushing the clumsy customer toward an exit. You remember later that there was no odor, no electricity in the air at all, that it was as empty of flavor as the customers were of spirit, and that above the strained quiet was the sound of hard objects being rubbed, like teeth grating together.

On the third floor you are greeted very cordially by a smiling guide who gives you a warm handshake. Dressed in street clothes, he wears a name plate bearing the name Al. The neat sign over the entrance states unimposingly, Rehabilitation Department.

"Well, this is it," he says, seeming to know that this is what you've been looking for. "Browse around. I know we'll have something you can use."

It isn't crowded. The wares are piled high in rather disorganized bundles on the counter tops. In fact, there are none of the ready-made kits that you found on the lower floors. You ask Al about this.

"It would be easier, I suppose, to market our wares that way," he answers, "but it wouldn't do our customers much good. What they purchase means much more to them if they can pick out just the articles that are of specific use to them. And no one counter is stocked with a complete set of made-to-wear items; the customer has to put them together himself.

"For instance, over there at the Reading Counter he can pick up something that will go well with what he gets from the Good Books section, and the two items will harmonize beautifully with a bolt or two of material from the Discussion Group counter. Or he might find a length of chain gears in the Job Training corner that will mesh easily with the sprockets he'll find in the Preparing For The Future corner. And, of course, no one who comes through is really complete without selected patterns from our Personal Hygiene and Good Manners stock, though sometimes we have to push these a little harder than some of the others."

Something, you know, is missing. "Where are the floorwalkers? The other floors were lousy with them."

"Oh, they're around," Al answers. "Only here they

don't wear uniforms, and their job is to help a customer who is undecided pick out colors that won't clash when he tries to put them together. Then, too, there aren't many of them, since we don't have a shoplifting problem." Above the conversational hubbub, the rhythm of rock music bounces along. The air smells fresh, invigorating.

"This is great!" you blurt out happily. "On my next visit, I'll come straight up here. No need to stop at . . ."

Al shakes his head sadly. "I'm sorry. You can't do that."

"What? Why not?"

"It is impossible to come directly to Rehabilitation from Anarchy. The elevator automatically stops on the Control level, and it is timed to spend an interval there before it proceeds to our department."

"But can't you fix it so that it makes an express run?"

"That's been tried. No way. There's something in the way these stores are built that prevents an express run from Anarchy to Rehabilitation. I'm truly sorry about that—I can't stand the tension in Control, either. But we have to grit our teeth and bear it for as long as it takes to get that elevator moving again."

You are thunderstruck—speechless.

"A few stores," Al goes on, "a very, very few build only one story, at ground level."

"Ah, and it's Rehabilitation!" you exclaim, brightening.

"No, hate to dash your hopes. But it's just as often an Anarchy or Control store. It all depends on what the owner's selling."

The rather weird tour you just went on is representative of the three possible states that relations among the boys can assume, depending on what *you* as counselor are selling. The only difference between your dorm and the department store is that all your customers are the same people and that the character of the department can change rather abruptly from one to another. In other words, the atmosphere can be one of control when you arrive at seven in the morning and anarchy by seven twenty, or anarchy when you get there and, if things go right, control ten minutes later. But, as Al says, it is impossible to transform the emotional tone from anarchy directly to rehabilitation for the simple reason that you can't sell self-improvement if you can't even get their attention. The unfortunate thing about most detention homes is that the relations elevator is forever stalled somewhere between anarchy and control, depending on the strength of the counselor. Let us turn, then, from this allegorical treatment to some of the actual stops, breakdowns, and slippages of your little cable car.

Your goal at the outset is to get your charges to help you manage them and then to move on, depending on their readiness for it, to their governing themselves. Now this is an easy thing to say; in fact, sociologists and psychologists, and the more enlightened institutional directors have been preaching it for thirty years. But the difference between saying it and doing it is so vast and seemingly so difficult that in most juvenile centers the group leaders have assumed a to-hell-with-it attitude and fallen back on the old, nonproductive anarchy-control treadmill. Why? Simply because there is usually little administrative support for it and primarily because no one has successfully explained—in plain language—how that relations elevator can be hauled up to the top floor. The result? Rehabilitation through self-government has become the Ford Edsel of institutional life.

Finally, before we get into the how's of elevator operation, let me admit that I of necessity am rather rough on administrators and occasionally take a shot at my fellow counselors, even while acknowledging that both groups are mired in the same pool of bureaucratic quicksand. An alert and skeptical reader might justifiably entertain the question whether the author was the perfect counselor or anywhere near it. Are you kidding? As a counselor I made enough mistakes and boneheaded misjudgments to write a book. And here it is. Humbly, it is intended to be your shortcut around that wasteland of a million pitfalls into most of which I managed to stumble.

3.   TAKING HOLD—PART I

Your first task is to get that elevator off the Anarchy level, if that is where it is when you arrive on the scene. By definition this means that you have to establish control, which is a form of relations in which brutalities, thefts, homosexual assaults, and bullying are brought to a halt. This can be a tall order, particularly if the behavior has become firmly engrained in dormitory life, and even more so if other counselors on the shifts following or preceding yours seem to be tolerant of it. In other words, violence can become a group habit; it can settle into a dormitory like stale sweat into an old shirt. And would you believe that I once worked in a center where it was the custom to put new and inexperienced counselors alone in a dormitory with boys who had just been admitted from the streets? The boys still had their bad habits, and the counselors, since they were untrained, had not yet worked out means for coping with violence and riot. This dormitory, "intake," turned out to be the graveyard of many a budding counselor's ambitions.

Group control has two origins: that which comes from you and that which comes from the boys. While the latter is the desired form, at the start it is you who must lay down the rules of regular conduct. Your little refugees aren't well enough organized to do it. Such organization as they have is designed to pay off only to those with the strongest muscles and the least restraint in using them. If dormitory security is a lottery prize, the toughest boys always have the winning tickets; in fact, the *only* tickets.

The Relations Method operates on both levels of group control. On this level, in which you are the controlling force, the counselor makes use of a boy's sensitivity about the way his peers think of him to induce him to behave in a particular way. For instance, if a youngster knows that all the boys in his dorm are turned off by a particular hang-up of his, such as not bathing, the human drive for approval and the human dislike for group hostility will usually get him into the shower. The only qualification for this rule is that his sensitivity to group feeling, or his social consciousness, must be acute and tuned in on the wave length of dormitory feeling.

The sense in this approach is, in simple terms, that it gives each boy a role as keeper of the peace and group standards rather than a violator, as an upholder of his own dignity and that of his peers and, most importantly, as a formulator of generally accepted standards of good behavior rather than one of their detractors. In short, a shot at a new, improved social function and, if the lesson sticks, a chance at a new personal identity. The word lesson is used purposely, for as a counselor you are, in fact, a teacher and what you hope to demonstrate is that they, as inheritors of the human spirit, have within them the capacity to work out their salvation, first as a group, then as breathing, functioning individuals. Now all this is third-floor stuff and as Al said, we first must spend an interval on the Control level. So let us press the proper button, open the elevator door and meet again that strait-laced fellow in the gold-braided monkey suit.

The place to begin group control is in a group meeting, a rather formal assembly in which all the boys on your roster as well as all the counselors on your shift assemble in the dormitory. Let's say that up to now your boys have been allowed to do as they please, that is, turn the dormitory into a pretty good facsimile of hell. A good time for the meeting is after breakfast and before starting the morning chores. Breakfast was chaotic and the place looks like Central Park after a peace riot. No one shows any inclination to clean up; they are all lounging around, throwing darts, playing checkers, doing anything evasive of work. When you call them together, you describe in pungent language (no profanity, please) exactly how the joint looks. Be matter-of-fact, but emphasize what you have to say with descriptive terms like junkyard and pigsty. Remind them that even though a building may be brand new and the furnishings right out of the factory, it won't take long for it to resemble a sewer if the people occupying it are slovenly. Do not threaten to withhold lunch or any meal at any time. You can't get away with it. While you may personally feel that it would be an excellent object lesson in the building of a relationship between working and eating, if you were hauled into court by some parents or civil watchdogs, they would pin your ears back. That the same boy may grow into a man who doesn't recognize the link between working and eating seems not to bother them. So don't try it.

Now there are two reasons why your strong opening was necessary. If unsanitary conditions have existed in the dorm for a long time, many of the boys have become accustomed to it, so that now the sight of unmade beds and a littered floor no longer disturbs them. What you have done has jarred them awake and shown them how far from accepted standards of cleanliness and order they have drifted. If the other counselors have peacefully coexisted with this state of affairs, in other words, have encouraged it by their failure to condemn and correct it, the boys will resent you—at first—for barging in with your biting criticism. The second reason is that you are putting them on notice that you are a counselor who gives a damn about how they live and what goes on among them and that you are willing to stick out your neck and make judgments about the quality of their behavior and their surroundings.

Criticism of a situation without a suggestion of a remedy is futile; in fact, it is worse than saying nothing. So your next step should go something like this: "Boys, I've told you how lousy the beds look; now I'm going to demonstrate the right way to make them up so that the corners are sharp and the spread doesn't look as though someone is having a nightmare under it." Then pull a bed to the center of the floor and, with all of them looking .on, make it up. Yeah, *you,* the counselor. Maybe you don't know it, but some of your little refugees have never made a bed in their lives. Some of them have never *had* a bed in their lives. The part that is hardest for them to catch on to at first is the "hospital corner," so do that little operation two or three times. Of course, there are several styles of bedmaking, so whatever yours is, make sure that everyone gets on to it. Then, "This is the way it's supposed to look when you get finished. You ought to be able to bounce a quarter three feet high off that spread. Now, let's see who can put together the best-looking cot!" Most of them, if not all, will hop to it and upon finishing will come and ask for inspection. What they really want is approval. If the bed is correctly done, you should be as liberal in your praise as you were severe in criticizing.

"Say, here's a beauty, everyone! Let's see if anybody can top this!" With this beginning you have given them the opportunity to earn the one thing without which hope for further improvement is impossible, a sense of achievement.

Will all of them fall in line behind this little maneuver? Probably not, but right now you're thinking of your boys as a group of people, and I've never seen less than ninety-five per cent cooperation with this approach. Ninety-five per cent success in any game is damn good. Incidentally, there are counselors who don't know how to make a bed properly. If you are one of these, kindly check in at the infirmary and ask a nurse to show you how. It could be that your supervisor won't know either.

In your opening remarks, you created a sense of awareness among them about their living so comfortably amid untidiness (if that is the area of concern of your first meeting). You caused them to see through your eyes the dormitory squalor and they moved to correct it. Whatever impelled them to action will carry over, if only briefly, to general cleaning routines. Incidentally, it is difficult to overstate the importance to the general institutional population of the maintenance of personal habits of cleanliness. Never mind the fact that it is a good character trait to develop. Think of the havoc that could be raised by an epidemic of "crabs" among the boys (itching and odor in the crotch due to fungal growth), or an invasion of the dormitories by rats looking for uncollected food and places to nest and multiply. The counselor who nags about soap, water, and the scrub brush ain't just whistlin' "Dixie."

One of the most mysterious and gratifying phenomena I have witnessed is that boys who are particularly mischievous or obnoxious in other aspects of dormitory life often turn out to be the best workers. I can recall a youth who was, in fact, psychotic, with uncontrollable aggressiveness. He was the first out of bed every morning and made it up perfectly, kept his locker immaculate and always volunteered to clean the room. The rest of the day, though, he gave us unrelieved hell.

The opening exercise that you and your boys just went through is the start of control as it originates from the counselor. It was you who found the form unfit and you who set the standard for future cleanliness. I don't want to give the impression that things always go as neatly as the above would suggest. At the writing of this section, I had been working for a week with a particularly unresponsive crew who, it turned out, needed stronger doses of counselor-initiated controls than I had been coming on with. In my experience, it is far better to err on the side of strictness than on that of leniency, because in the former case the pressure can be eased. It's much tougher sledding to go in the other direction.

An important transference must now take place. Your concern for neatness and order must somehow become their concern. Your pride in well-made beds and clean floors must become their pride. How is this accomplished? Of several acceptable ways, the best I know is through consistency and reinforcement.

Consistency is the degree of predictability you show in your everyday dealings with the group. Your attitude must become one of the new mooring places to which their emotional tendencies can be tied. For instance, if one day you raise holy ned about the way the dorm looks and the next day you let them slide by on the same offense, or if one day you allow a free-for-all and the next you rave and rant if one little rascal so much as frowns at another, you will undermine whatever controls you have managed to establish. Moreover, you will introduce an element of confusion and frustration among the boys that will in the long run be as bad as anarchy itself.

Of course, you are not the only possible source of this inconsistency. Allowance must be made for the man who relieves you or who works the shift before yours. It could be that he is one of those zombies I spoke of in the beginning; you know, anything goes so long as they don't disturb his television program or interfere with the records he's listening to. At one group meeting, a youngster brought this sharply to my attention: "Mr. So-and-So never gives us any trouble about this. He doesn't bother us at all, so what are you bitching so much about?" Your answer to this is that you are not Mr. So-and-So and that you care very much about what they do and that if they cooperate with you, they will not be bothered or bitched at on your shift either.

Reinforcement is the strengthening of a desired pattern of behavior through reward and praise. When the boys comply, you should not be stingy with compliments and, depending on the facilities and monies available in your center, some extension of privileges should be offered, such as an extra movie, a party, treats, and the like. And, of course, for it to stick, reinforcement must be consistent.

It is to be expected that there will be a certain amount of disharmony between the way you manage the group and the way other people do. This is unfortunate and is the inevitable outgrowth of the lack of management planning among ninety-nine per cent of today's youth houses. In other words, counselors are allowed to freelance in their custodial methods without regard for coordination, cohesion, or continuity with the other shifts. The most frequent alibi I have heard counselors use for these wide disparities is: "There is no one way to handle children." That may be true, but some ways are much better than others, and it behooves any youth-center director to attempt to structure a method and training that will bring some consistency to the direction of dormitory life and reduce the need for the boys to readjust their thinking and behavior every time the shift changes. For example, in the matter of cursing, there may be great differences in the sensitivity of counselors to it, ranging all the way from the counselor himself swearing at the boys to the righteous indignation of a real puritan. Personally, I think it is a good idea to eschew profanity for a number of reasons. One is that a mouth spewing garbage is one of those self-belittling residues that stubbornly hangs on to the boys after they have come in from the street, a trait that is usually mobilized to the disservice of someone else. On this basis alone, it should be condemned. Another indictment of it is that you are trying to encourage among your youngsters the habit of thinking through the things they are saying and thereby improving their ability to communicate with others in a respectful, intelligent manner. The use of discourse that is permeated with profanity is a good sign that there is very little going on between the speaker's ears and that his thoughts are as barren as his vocabulary. Would you believe that in one center where I worked, the boys under nine learned most of their vulgar phrases and curse words from the counselors themselves?

To resolve problems such as this, there should be conversations or conferences with the other group leaders. These meetings should be coordinated, in fact, insisted upon by the administration. Don't count on it. The fact is that you will probably have to initiate them yourself. It won't make you popular, but popularity was never a conscientious counselor's long suit anyway.

Even though at first you are thinking of the boys as a collective unit, their individual material needs must be met and met consistently if you are to hold down the grumbling. What these needs are is rather easy to delineate. They are the same as yours. Think of the things you use upon arising in the morning, and they are exactly what your boys want: towel, washcloth, toothbrush, toothpaste, soap, access to a mirror and hot water. The exceptions are those boys whose home life was so deprived that they seldom saw any of these articles, let alone learned how to use them.

I can recall one group of thirteen boys to whom we had to issue thirty-six toothbrushes over a two-week period. No, they weren't wearing them out on their ivories; they found out that they made excellent shoe-polish applicators and to hell with their teeth. As the youngest of them was over thirteen, it follows then that it isn't enough just to hand some of your little refugees the goods and say, "Go use it." The facts of life in the city jungle are such that you may actually have to demonstrate some morning exactly what a toothbrush (or a comb or soap) is for.

To summarize the idea of transference in the building

of good relations within the group: once you have awakened in them the sense of being a participant in an important group enterprise, that is, the maintenance of friendly interrelations, sanitary conditions, mutual trust, you have truly begun to take hold. This is usually not an overnight process, although you will be surprised at how often it seems that way.

Group sentiment is a powerful psychic force. Once you have transferred your concerns to them, you can use that to sustain their good performances in their assigned tasks. For example, if on a particular morning there are two or three chores left undone and you know who the malingerers are, it should no longer be necessary to address them by name to prod them into action. You simply call to the attention of the group that someone's bed is still wrinkled or a couple of lockers are in disarray, making the dorm look bad. The boys will do the rest. They move much faster under the prodding of their peers than they ever will for you.

Does this work with every group and with every youngster in every group? Nope. But the ones who are refractory to this approach are few and far between. What, then, are the sources of failure? Moreover, how do you know when you have failed? When, in other words, should you hang the label of failure on your attempts to arouse group pride in the surroundings and induce participation in the efforts to improve them?

The answers to these questions are extremely difficult to come by, because counselors have different standards by which they rate their own performances. For example, a guy who considers himself to be a real hotshot might feel that if his boys aren't up and cracking the moment he enters the dorm after a few days of using this approach, he has somehow missed the boat. Another fellow with a much more modest self-estimate might struggle along for weeks without noticeable improvement and still not pronounce the enterprise a dud. Both of them could be right; or they might just as well be wrong. The missing factor is the consideration of the character of the kids you are dealing with. In general, the more mature your boys are, the less time will be needed to organize their concern and transference. Be aware that maturity has little to do with age, although age may have a great deal to do with maturity. I have had eight-year-olds who were mature enough to vote in any general election. I have had seventeen-year-olds who, in terms of readiness for life, should never have been allowed out of the crib.

A second consideration in our answer is the presence of severely disturbed boys in the dorm. Many of the refugees from the city jungle are somewhat bruised, but some of them, like the sociopath, can be real dillies. This is the lad who can't stand institutions, the laws and strictures that regulate the activities of most of the rest of us. Now he sees you building up around him just such restraints as he acted against on the outside. He finds it hard to function in that setting, and if there are several such individuals in your group, the time needed for you to "take hold" will be somewhat extended. He's always the last out of bed, last to find his clothes, last in the shower, always losing his toothbrush, usually truant from school or the dorm, and so on. You should be suspicious whenever it appears that this guy seems to be involved with every breaking of a rule. Consult his folder, social worker, teacher, your supervisor, or any other source for in-depth information on him. He isn't hopeless. It just takes longer for peer pressure to get to him. And if you have five or six at one time out of a population of only fourteen or fifteen, group sentiment may become a will-o'-the-wisp that you never catch up to. In other words, they constitute too large a fraction of the total population to be swayed into compliance by what the law abiders believe in. Get ready for some long days, because you're going to have to tackle them one-on-one. Of course, your supervisor could help you by considering a couple of transfers or trades with another group; but don't count on anything.

Boys who are emotionally disturbed, psychotic, or mentally retarded often could care less which way the winds of dormitory sentiment are blowing. In the last case, they may not even be aware that there is such feeling. Although these are extreme examples, the counselor would do well to take these into consideration when he is assessing the degree of success or failure of his approach. There are many types of emotional disturbance and the presence of one of them in a particular boy is, of course, more important than whether he goes along with the games people play.

Any widely disparate behavior that is potentially harmful to the boy himself or to his peers, or that is consistently disruptive of dormitory life, should be noted and reported. While you are not a psychologist, there are cues and hints by which a serious disturbance will occasionally make its presence known. For instance, an unrelenting aggressiveness directed toward the other boys or the counselor that is not triggered by material needs, revenge, or any external provocation but seems to stem from some inner need to "act out" against the world should give the alert counselor cause to ask for a psychological evaluation.

Another clue is morbid self-interest, often accompanied by long spells of depression, which prevents him from being concerned with such external enterprises as games, chores, school, conversation, even eating, and which should cause the alert group leader to have second thoughts about his potential for group assimilation. And if the depression is punctuated by little episodes of self-destructive acts, such as burning himself with a cigarette or scratching himself with a nail or pencil so that he draws blood, or a tendency toward accidents, look out! More than one suicide victim has thus tried to tip off the world that he was looking for an exit.

The other side of the coin from the standpoint of outward signs is the "happiness kid," who is going to be visited any day now by his long-missing mother or father, and for whom every day in the home is a joy forever; he just loves everything about it, including its crowdedness and monotony; whose unrelieved euphoria is matched only by his ineffectiveness in carrying out the easiest chores assigned to him and by his low tolerance for disappointment. I observed one such youngster, an eleven-year-old, provoked into a chair-throwing rage when a pair of socks he had washed and dried disappeared from the radiator. A week later, he repeated the performance when the totally imaginary scheduled visit of his parents did not materialize.

4. TAKING HOLD—PART II

The conditions under which you are expected to wreak your miracles vary greatly from one city to another, and even among institutions under the same city administration there is a wide variance of physical facilities and personnel competency. In New York City, for example, one facility recently brought to public notoriety featured jammed, smelly dormitories, rampant drug use, and inmate abuse, while right across town is capacious Jennings Hall, where there are two boys to a comfortable room, a counselor ratio of one for every twelve youngsters, and administrators who seem to give a damn about the effectiveness of their rehabilitation program. And in the same city, somewhere between the two aforementioned centers in quality of service is one whose population census and whose level of demonstrated efforts to provide a habitable environment for New York's no deposit–no return children rises and falls with the heat of newspaper exposes. When the heat is on, that is, when fed-up employees take to the sidewalks before television reporters (God bless 'em), the creaking, scarred floors are given a rush wax job, vacancies are miraculously located for the languishing youngsters, new spreads materialize out of thin air for the beds, long-neglected plumbing is suddenly wrenched into working order, and someone even takes a stab at making the menu palatable.

It takes a loudly squeaking wheel (and crusading journalists) to shake money loose from state and city treasuries and wide-awake administrators to use wisely those tiny improvements that are granted. There are few things that you as an individual counselor can do to influence this total picture. Anyway, we are concerned here with improving your functioning regardless of conditions.

The first several pages of "Taking Hold" were

concerned with a primary approach to dormitory control. We may now become more specific. To begin with, taking hold depends as much on proper counselor attitude as it does on the possession of an armamentarium of techniques. In short, you have to be awake. That isn't as obvious a first step as it may seem. I don't mean *just* awake in the sense that your eyes are open and you're able to light your cigarette without burning your nose. That much we must take for granted. What is required is that you be the eyes, ears, and nose of your dorm. You have to overhear conversations—not exactly eaves-dropping—and see any hostile glares between two boys, pick up a word, a sentence, a voice inflection. You have to know the signs of drug abuse: unexplained tiredness, lethargy, sudden bursts of manic activity—particularly after unexplained absences, glassy eyes, pinpoint pupils, a funny-smelling cigarette, stitchwork on the arms, a spell of runny nose. Your antenna must always be up for mood swings, individual or group, a gradual or rapid increase in thefts or missing items. In other words, have your mental vane up for the way the winds are blowing in your dorm; the kids will tip you off without knowing it or meaning to. If they've been getting up pleasantly but this morning they wake up grousing and bitching, you're going to have to adjust, perhaps give them more rope than usual until you discover what put the burr up their behinds. You don't have to be Sherlock Holmes to keep a step ahead of them. All I'm saying is look and listen.

As an example of how sharp ears can ward off a fight, let's look at a case history of what I consider to be a good counselor in action. In a certain New York children's home, a counselor overheard a Negro youngster, whom we'll call Rufus, mutter, "Spanish motherfucker." Now the use of motherfucker as a name isn't necessarily serious; what pricked up the counselor's ears was the use of racial identification with it. It is, incidentally, an irony among these types of boys that deep-seated, fighting anger is heralded by racial terms. That is, if you are a white counselor and one of your youngsters refers to you simply as a bastard, prick, faggot or what have you, he's only moderately angry, or perhaps even teasing. It's when you become a *white* bastard or prick that he is showing real hostility. Anyway, the counselor looked at the boy, said nothing, and kept going (remembering, however, who it was). When they lined up for dinner, he saw Rufus leave his place in line and go stand in front of a Puerto Rican, who stared sullenly back at him. Again the counselor said nothing, but he began to keep a closer watch on both of them. An indifferent group leader would have paid no attention, but you already have the three ingredients necessary for an explosion: two obviously hostile boys and proximity.

When the group arrived at the dining hall, the Puerto Rican youngster sat next to a friend and mumbled something in Spanish. (This is something else the observant counselor should mark: when angry Latin boys who are fluent in English begin to mutter among themselves in Spanish. It does not mean necessarily that they are up to anything; it could be entirely innocent. It's just another straw in the wind that you should note.) Now the more aggressive Rufus hassled the boy's friend out of his seat and sat down next to him. You could have parked a Mafioso's Cadillac on the hatred in the air between them. At this point, the counselor did something very simple and very effective. He rose, walked over to their table and took the seat next to them, giving each a long, inquiring look. A quiet dinner was had by all.

When the group returned to the dorm, he called them both over to a corner and listened to their stories. He helped them settle the difference—a dispute over a missing sweater—without involving the rest of the dorm and without the fight ever taking place. A simple, commonplace exercise? It is if handled right. But compare this treatment with the difficulty of having to break up a general riot among, say, twenty boys and I think you will see my point.

Let us, for the sake of argument, suppose that the fight somehow came off while you were doing something more important than watching your boys, like making out your weekly jellybean-allotment request. You were detained by the supervisor, who demanded that you do the request over; seems that you forgot to specify how many beans of each color you wanted (more trivial demands have been made, believe me). When you get back to the dorm, Rufus and his foe have organized their friends into warring camps and a dorm-wrecking riot rages. What do you do?

Some years ago, I was confronted with a situation very similar to this one. My first move was for the supervisor, because in this case two dorms were arrayed against each other and the hallway connecting them looked like no man's land. She declined to come. So I went back alone. Fortunately I have a big mouth—I mean a loud voice—which enabled me to shout them down with statements like, "Cut it out!" "Put down that chair!" and "Let him go!" At first I was surprised that they stopped without my having to grab any of them; then I remembered that whenever two boys or two groups of boys are fighting, at least one side wants someone to break it up, and if both parties are scoring heavily, *everybody* is relieved to see you hustling onto the scene.

I may as well confess that when I see a bully getting what has been a long time coming to him, I travel a little slower than usual. This is poor practice; your job is to prevent and break up fights, not referee or, worse yet, enjoy them. But then, I never said I was an angel; it's a human frailty that needs correcting. Anyway, after I had got the boys settled down and cleaning up the littered arena, my supervisor sauntered in and handed me a paper to sign. When I read it, I realized why she had been too busy to come view the high jinks. She had spent the time writing out a disciplinary report on *me* for an allegation a boy had made the day before that I had paddled him. It does not matter that the charge was false. What does matter is that this is the way some supervisors will ride out a crisis. Get the picture? In fairness, I should add that such administrators are rare, but one on a staff is plenty.

Getting back to you, once you have quieted them down, don't start in immediately with an exploratory meeting. Their tempers are still too hot for a rational discussion, and all you'll get are charges and countercharges. So stop the relations elevator on the control floor for awhile.

Identify the walking wounded and give them passes to the infirmary if it seems that they need it. Busy work will come in handy now, like cleaning up the battleground. If some refuse to help, don't insist; let them stew in silence. The last thing you need at this point is a hassle between you and an already angry boy. It is important, though, that you stay close to the battlers who seem the angriest. After thirty minutes or so of relative quiet, you may start your conciliation meeting, plying them with some pointed questions about who did what to whom and *why*. They'll tell you what the score is and the cause of their beef.

Let us scramble the picture a bit more. Suppose that the riot is in full flower, your supervisor is working on that report about you, and your shouting is having about as much effect on your boys as the playboy mouse had on the prostitute elephant. Like nothing, dad. One thing you could do is join your supervisor and refuse to go back until he or she accompanies you. This drops the buck solidly in his lap, where it belongs. Now he has to come and the two of you can return the dorm to sanity. But let us suppose, just to make the problem really sticky, that the guy has anticipated your move and left a note for you on his desk, saying something about having to see a sick cousin in Canarsie. Most detention homes have contingency plans for just this kind of screw-up. One of the more common ones is to telephone the switchboard and call for aid from other dorms. Or, if that is not forthcoming, you could call for police help, which usually arrives fairly promptly; local gendarmes react quickly to the magic words "detention home riot." Whatever you do, be sure you can identify the parties who started the little fandango, because they are the key to stopping it and preventing another, and they are the ones toward whom your postdisturbance counseling has to be aimed. It goes without saying that in your written report you should tell all that happened, including the events leading up to it, even if these events occurred days before. Mention the note your supervisor wrote.

A word of caution. Be very careful about stepping between two boys who seem to be going at each other like

Godzilla and Draco the Dragon, especially if you're new on the job. A case history will tell why.

At a center in Ohio a number of years ago, a mild-mannered counselor whom we'll call Smith, had charge of a special dorm for emotionally disturbed boys. He had recently been discharged from the Air Force, and this was his first civilian job. It was ten o'clock at night and the boys were presumably preparing for bed. One of the kids came to the office door and reported that a fight had broken out in the bathroom. Smith, working alone, dashed out of the office to the scene of the "fight." The boy who had brought the message then ripped the phone wires loose. Of course, you know what happened when the counselor reached the john and jumped between the boys "slugging" each other. They and about five others grabbed him and played "Dixie" on his skull with a mop wringer and took his keys. The dorm was empty of everybody except poor Smith when the midnight relief man came. I'll say one thing for the guy, though. He was all compassion. As the stretcher bearers were hauling him out to the ambulance, he kept muttering between blood-clotted lips, "Thank God, I didn't hit any of them; thank God, I didn't hit any of them." Smith's fault? Nope. He should have been saving his strength up to cream whoever made up the schedule to put a brand-new counselor alone in a setup like that. But as Nina Simone sings, "It be's that way sometimes."

5. TAKING HOLD—PART III

In order for the group-relations method of child improvement to work, the counselor must "know" his boys; that is, he must make an original estimate of them as a group of people on whom he hopes to leave a constructive impression. This is where the wakefulness spoken of earlier comes in handily. Even though the individual personalities represented will, of necessity, range over the entire spectrum of "normal" psyches, and may even include a psychopatholgy or two, there will be a prevailing collective nature that will express itself. In short, are they as a group sullen, lively, friendly, hostile, smart, slow, cooperative, balky, querulous, timid, aggressive, threatening, sly, or what? In addition, the alert counselor should be aware of group mood swings like collective expressions of disappointment or elation. This is a must if he is to be able to rate his effectiveness as an influence on group life. This first evaluation should not take a long time, nor is it particularly difficult. All the counselor has to do, conditions permitting, is to look and listen.

To be more specific, what are some of the signposts that one should read in order to get a line on this "collective personality"? The answer to this question is found by the counselor asking himself whether the boys are relatively easy to assemble for breakfast and other meals; how many times a day he has to break up fights or intervene in quarrels; the number of complaints he gets before noon about stolen articles; how many times he has to explain some new procedure before everyone catches on; how long it takes them to settle down at bedtime, and so on. Also, are they quiet and cooperative with you and little demons with the next group leader? Do they follow your instructions to the letter and turn into uncomprehending cabbages when someone else makes a simple request? Put in still another way: To what extent has steadily mature behavior been induced into attitudes that were previously negative, erratic, and self-destructive? While making your appraisal, bear in mind that we are talking about the change of an anti-social mixture of personalities into a community of mutually tolerant people. While, as I stated before, this preliminary view should not take a long time, there are several precautions to take if the counselor is not to fool himself, as a co-worker and I once did with a group of fifteen boys in a New York children's shelter.

Up to that time we had been blessed with "good" reputations as counselors who could get the boys to follow routine and house rules with a minimum of static. Mr. T., as I'll call him, was a young fellow who had worked in a Pittsburgh detention home where conditions were somewhat more martial than in New York: that is, the boys did as they were told and that was that. My Ohio background was similar.

In our new group, the population consisted of eleven Negro youths and four Puerto Ricans. Relatively speaking, it wasn't a bad bunch except for a low grade of intimidation of the Latins by the blacks. T. and I observed them for a couple of days, carrying them through their procedures without hassling them about the pranks that seemed always to fall on the Puerto Ricans, such as toothpaste being squirted into their shoes and the theft of some of their belongings. Our intentions were to find out whether the culprits were just one or two of the boys or all of the blacks in general before we made our move. They forced our hand, though, when we came in on the third day and learned that one of them had been jumped and slugged rather severely. The victim was the lightest-skinned of the blacks, with curly hair and a quiet, almost effeminate manner. So we started our group meetings.

As we had confidently expected (Mr. T. and I weren't modest), group behavior improved steadily over the next few days. Curly stopped coming to us with complaints, the Latin boys were no longer doused with toothpaste while they slept, and the dorm was kept a lot cleaner. By the fourth day of meetings, it appeared that the expected miracle had been wrought. The "cool daddy" counselors had done it again.

I congratulated myself and my partner.

He congratulated himself and me.

We congratulated our supervisor.

He congratulated the two of us.

And everybody went home feeling good.

Two days later, Curly ran away from the center, and when he was caught he refused to be reassigned to our dorm. The reason? A number of brutal beatings by three of the little mothers who had sat through the meetings saying "Right on, brother," and raising the clenched fist salute as though they agreed with everything we said. T. and I felt airsick as we plummeted from our lofty perch of self-esteem. The boys had conned us as if we were a couple of Times Square drunks.

What had happened? Without taking anything away from the boys in their clever deception, some things should have occurred to us immediately. A good rule for any child-care worker to follow is not to believe his or her own press clippings. You're never as good as your friends claim (nor as bad as some of your enemies might declare). In other words, Mr. T. and I were so ready to pat ourselves on the back that we set ourselves up for this fiasco like a couple of country rubes at the fair. Second, we took the new-found calm in the dorm at face value. Things were quiet on the surface, and we assumed that this was an accurate picture of the real state of affairs. Ordinarily I take aside a boy who has been having some difficulty and inquire about whether things have improved for him after a series of group meetings. With Curly I failed to do this. He stopped complaining, so we promptly forgot him. Third, the very fact of the sudden quiet in the dorm should have alerted us, for it was a quiet that seemed brooding and without life. Be assured that in a dorm filled with restless teenagers there is, or should be, no such thing as the kind of solemn absence of noise that descended on our quarters ... unless the kids are all on drugs. So the signs were all there; we just couldn't see them.

From this first general assessment of the social flavor in your group, you now go to the particular. One of the first things that comes to notice is the pecking order, that is, the dormitory hierarchy as determined by the boys, usually according to whom they consider to be the toughest physically (exactly the way large "enlightened" nations decide on the division of new territories). The best seat for viewing television, the biggest helping at the dinner table, the fact of never having things stolen from him and of never being without a more or less willing creditor is the happy lot of the top man in the pecking order. The lower positions are assumed in order of their occupants' expected or demonstrated ability to defend them. In not a few cases the top boy will on the basis of friendship assign a higher spot to someone who could not attain it on his own strength. In just as many cases, this patronage is based on money, the well-known protection racket, another page out of the grown-up book of social management (and out of our State Department's book of international relations).

One such instance was brought to my attention during a stay at a New York home. On the days that we handed out their allowances, we noticed that one of the smaller boys, a curly-haired Spanish kid whose feuding parents couldn't decide what to do with him, was quickly sought out by one or two of the larger boys and was immediately thereafter stone broke. When we asked him why he was so popular with some of his peers on payday, he answered that he owed them money for little "favors" they had done for him. He declined to tell what those "favors" were. And, as it usually does with the protection-racket victim, word got around that Juan was an easy touch for "knuckle money," and each week the number of his "protectors" increased. And, as always happens, the Saturday came when little Juan couldn't pay. And, as it always does, this made his "protectors" mad. And, as they always do, his "protectors" began to pound him. And, as they will sometimes do, the victim blew the whistle on them. I might add parenthetically that it takes tremendous courage for a protection-racket victim to squeal on his tormentors, whether he is a little boy in a detention home or an old man trying to run a delicatessen in Brooklyn. In either case, the complainant runs the terrible risk of indifference or disbelief from the authorities (in some neighborhoods, the racketeers *are* the authorities), which leaves him naked in the storm of his "protectors'" fury. Read *The People Vs. Blutcher,* by Eliot Asinof, for more insight into this grim situation on the adult level.

In any dormitory, the evidence for the existence of the protection game is usually pretty obvious. Large boys who never seem to be without money, payday popularity of certain smaller boys, chronic poverty among these same small fellows, and most significantly, a dogged closemouthedness about the flow of money in the dormitory seem to be the hallmarks of this trade. An interesting parallel between dormitory life and commercial life on the outside is shown by the fact that if the counselor simply follows the trail of money transactions, they, like Hansel and Gretel's pebbles, will usually lead him out of his forest of ignorance about what goes on among the boys. *Watch for pay-offs*—because they are made not only for "protection," but also for homosexual favors, drugs, silence about plans for escape or assaults, and so on. And when the counselor spots a money exchange, he should *always* find out what it's for. A good rule of thumb is to ask—privately—the guy who is doing the shelling out—soon after he has shelled out. He just may be disgruntled enough to give you the straight story if there's anything illegal about it. But, as with everything else, the state of relations that exists between you and the youngster will have the biggest influence on whether he lets you in on anything.

In the episode described above, the boy had to be assured that he would be safe from any reprisals at the hands of the boys who had been "protecting" him before he would give us any of the details about their racket. When we found out, we went a step further. We added insult to their injury by deducting enough instalments from their allowances to equal the amount they had gouged from Juan. This was, of course, simple justice and did not go beyond that to, say, punitiveness. Punitiveness is seldom educational, and it is growth that you as counselors are aiming for, not mere punishment. Therefore, a full airing of the incident at the next group meeting was held in order to motivate the "protectors" on the deeper level of an object lesson. No one likes to have the dirty linen of his behavior waved aloft in an assembly of his peers and former victims.

If the level of trust between the staff and the boys had been higher, we might have been told about the above situation far sooner by a youngster who was not involved. The importance of these "good vibrations" between counselors and kids cannot be overemphasized, as the following case episode will show.

In an Ohio diagnostic center one night in the spring of '69, a newly admitted white boy fellated ("sucked off") the whole dorm. He went from bed to bed taking on all comers (no pun intended). We would never have found it out if one of the boys who was later disgusted with himself had not told us. The code of silence would have forever kept him from our knowledge, which is exactly what had happened in the places from which he had been transferred. There was no mention of his weakness in his folder. When we found it out it was, of course, necessary to isolate him from the group and refer him to the ministrations of the resident psychologist. He was eventually removed entirely from the dorm and placed in a smaller group of youngsters, where closer supervision was possible. This is the best alternative of those that are available to you as a "nonprofessional" group leader. The smaller the group, the better the supervision; the better the supervision, the easier it is to deal with ringers like our friend above or "protectors." Be assured that most of the time there won't be anyone in your place to whom boys with psychotic or psychoneurotic problems can be shuttled for residential care. Oh, there'll be a psychologist or psychiatric social worker or two around, but I'm a betting man and I'm willing to give odds that the amount of time these persons have to work with any one youngster, to say nothing of the facilities your shelter provides for these services is, like zero. It's not their fault. It's just that America hasn't got serious yet about rehabilitation or the care of our no deposit-no return children.

For me to say that you are helpless when confronted by the emotionally disturbed or retarded child simply because you don't have a lot of spaghetti behind your name would be to deny the intent, indeed, the philosophy, of this book. Provided that he is not *completely* gone (and this can be hard to determine), there is much that you and your group can do to aid such an unfortunate. This is discussed in the final section.

6. STARTING THE DAY

Here is one of the major determinants of the kind of atmosphere you will be able to establish for the entire day: the way you get them up in the morning. The worst way is to shout or literally kick them out of bed. I have witnessed this being done and have done it myself enough times to be well aware of the probable outcome. While it is true that they may all tumble out a lot faster than for a counselor who uses less forceful methods, what you wind up with is a bunch of bickering, querulous little characters who will take out their resentment of you on each other. Compare the number of arguments, accusations, threats and near-fights that erupt on such mornings with the quieter emotional tone that follows a slower, less aggressive awakening, in which you come in, turn on the lights, speak in a pleasant voice, read the night man's notes while they gradually come to, re-enter and nudge the still unconscious ones with no more force than is necessary to bring them around, and so on.

I am not being doctrinaire in these instructions. If your group is on the anarchy level, you probably will have to go into your "tough" bag to get them up, in which case we can forget about the pleasant voice. But in your first group meeting, getting-up procedure should be high on the list of things to discuss.

The question might be asked: If counselors are aware of the advantages of the quiet beginning, why do so many continue in the old self-defeating technique? The answer has three facets: habit, schedule, and reputation. Some counselors are, like boys, slaves to habit. The shortest, most direct route to the desired response is to dump the sleepy guy out on the floor. It's difficult to sleep on that cold tile, especially if you've hit it with a brusk thump. And once the new counselor becomes spoiled by the ease of this method, it quickly becomes the biggest item in his bag and he begins to pull it out the minute he hits the dorm. The old formula of coincidence plus effect plus repetition equals habit takes hold and the detention home has another hooked counselor.

Secondly, most people who work within a system soon come to know of that system's demand that all parts of it march in lockstep to a prearranged sequence of activities called the schedule. There is a time, for instance, when the boys of Dorm B-1 are supposed to report for showers, and deviation by five or ten minutes from that expectation is regarded as a threat to efficiency; and there is a time when they are to show up for breakfast, and lateness throws the cafeteria into chaos, and a time for gym and for school and social service and so on.

Schedule comes to be viewed religiously, with something approaching awe, and the counselor who best fits his boys' movements into its niches and recesses like the interlocking pieces of a puzzle acquires the flattering reputation of a "good, tough" group leader. Like everyone else, I love a good reputation. What I am asking you to do is, if you've earned yours this way, to audit very carefully the cost of it—to the boys. For example, a boy who arrives at breakfast full of bile isn't much going to enjoy the meal to begin with: his Frosty Flakes will go down like broken glass. Schedule be damned, he jumps up and squares off the moment someone spills milk on his brotherhood button. And on Sunday, what good is getting them to the church on time if when they get there the only way they'll take the Lord's name is with a "damn" connected to it? The cost of your "good" reputation is prohibitive if you add to the debit side the hurt feelings, bruised knuckles, and the insidious strain on your nervous system of combating the tense dormitory atmosphere for eight hours.

I'm not putting down control or the adherence to a time schedule, for these are the tracks along which any bureaucracy must run. What I am saying is play the odds. And the odds are that getting the boys up in a fairly decent mood gives that much more weight to your attempts to exercise control in the early going.

What about the kid who won't get up no matter what? Should you strong-arm the little character? Maybe throw a glass of ice-cold water into his face? Tempting, isn't it? Don't do it. It isn't necessary. Carry out your routine with the rest of the group. Missing a privilege or two and group pressure will usually bring him around. One such fellow told me that his counselor would tickle his feet on mornings when he was a little slow to hit the deck. I endorse this. There's no better way to make someone get up smiling.

7. CAPPING THE VOLCANO

Group control need not begin with cleaning routines or with chores. The important rule is to start with something simple, something that will pay dividends in a hurry. Say, mealtime behavior. Until now they have been eating according to their old street etiquette, that is, the fastest hands and brawniest muscles get the choice cuts of meat, the extra dessert, the second helping. This is what all the shouting is about; the little mothers are being starved out by the big ones. Not only that, but the big boys may duck out when time comes to clean up. Now what you have to do is demonstrate that everyone can get enough to eat while exercising good manners and fair play toward the next guy. But you don't put it that way. You let them tell you. Here's how.

After the meal, when they are settling down in front of the TV, you step up to it, turn it off and say, "Boys, I want to ask you a few questions," or something to that effect. Incidentally, turning off the television set is a rather handy signal that you are displeased even though your voice is calm.

"Did anyone notice anything wrong with the way we ate?" I can guarantee that hands will shoot up and they'll tell you exactly what was wrong with it. What is more, half the guys who complain about mealtime behavior will be the very ones who stole food from their neighbors. They will defend it by stating that it's the only way they can be assured of getting enough to eat. It's not a willful lie, since they themselves believe it, and besides, it was the truth at home. Your next question is, "Now what is a better way to eat, in fact, the best way of all?" They will now give you the same list of proper ways to behave that you were going to run down to them. But the beautiful thing about this is that it came from them. Of course, your next question is whether there is anyone here who feels that he isn't man enough to abide by these wonderful suggestions that they have come up with. Only very rarely will someone admit that he's that kind of weakling; in fact, I've never seen it happen. Just before your next meal, you remind them of the promise *they* made, the standards *they* set, and that you want to see just what kind of men they are. It works. This is the relations technique at its best. The episode showed that you respected ideas formulated by them and, what is more important, summoned forth their potential for elevating their interpersonal relations to a higher and more sociable plane. One group of pre-teen youngsters who had been in the habit of waging a pier 6 brawl at the table spoke pridefully of how wonderful it was to eat their meals in peace and with mutual courtesy. "For the first time, there was some food left over, Mr. Henry," one of them told me.

I'm sure that for some counselors, the appearance of good table manners among their charges is small potatoes indeed, particularly if one has to hold a group meeting to achieve it. Don't kid yourself. Would you believe that this is the first time in the lives of many of them that they've asked for anything during a meal and tacked a "please" and "thank you" onto the ends of their request? And that it came as a shock to some of them that there actually *was* enough to go around without their having to slug somebody? Brother, they have climbed a mountain! And so have you if this is the first time you have used this approach to change their behavior. Now you must see that they don't tumble back down into their old habits, so you reinforce the change by praising them until it becomes a natural part of their group routine. Be sure to shore up this improvement by writing down what has happened in the daily log so that your relief man knows what's going on. Their new-found politeness may be too much for the poor guy if it comes as a complete surprise.

Let's move on to something a little stickier. One of the things contributing to a boy's misery in your dorm is the aggression he suffers at the hands of his fellows. Now this aggression may take any of several forms, from theft of his belongings to physical assault, and in some cases it may include gang rape. While these acts occur between individuals, they happen within the context of the dormitory setting, and it is the atmosphere of that setting that will finally determine whether you can bring these violations to a halt. In other words, if there is a spirit of anarchy in your dorm or classroom, there is no way that you can turn off the wellspring of cruelty. In fact, merely getting them out of bed will be a tough job—without the use of dynamite.

Let us suppose then that you know through rumors or

observation that the main bag in your dorm is "bogart-ing." To "bogart" someone is to take his possessions by direct threat or a sucker punch. Now, because of fear of re-prisal, the victims of these attacks aren't about to come to you with the names of the b-men. Their names would do you no good anyway, for it would only be one boy's word against another's. So at your next group meeting, you ask rather urgently, "Do you guys know how you should treat another human being? I mean, do you really know how to get along with each other?" Sure enough, the hands will rise and out will come the most beautiful descriptions of friendly relations you've ever heard. Here's the hooker! Half of them will come from the bogarters!

When you recover from shock, you ask, "Well, why don't you treat each other this way?"

Silence.

So you try another tack. "Is the way you've been treating one another the way you've just told me you should behave?"

"No."

"Why not?"

Silence.

"Is there anyone here who can tell how the way you treat each other is wrong?"

Your bogarters will tell you how; their victims are afraid to talk. One of the advantages of getting the boys to talk is that now you will hear about conditions that you never suspected existed, and they will feel secure in telling you because you haven't asked for names. And they will give you a bonus: they will tell you *why* they strong-arm the weaker boys. Need and habit. So simply by asking the right questions, you can discover what most of their hostile little acts are and possible remedies.

"We only take the things we need," one of them told me during a meeting I was holding in a New York center.

"You mean to tell me that if the center supplied you with the things you've been pulverizing the other kids for, you would stop?" The answer was, of course, yes; so I guaranteed the toothbrushes and talcum and candies, and extracted their promise to stop the sucker punching.

Almost all the boys who make a pledge like this will try to keep it; the guys on whom habit has too strong a grip are soon made conspicuous. It is on these hard-core malefactors that the aspect of group relations known as peer pressure must be applied. They are seldom more than two or three out of a population of twenty or so. In spite of them, there will be a noticeable fall-off in threats and sluggings, for which you should, of course, compliment the group.

I admit that the above sounds quite neat and simple. Bull! It's rarely that easy. But it is the direction the dialogue takes if you keep plying them with questions and letting them do most of the talking. I might add that the above exchange is an excerpt from a real case in which I was a participant in a New York center.

Now the problem remains of what to do with the unrepentant bully who doesn't feel bound by the consensus arrived at in the general discussion, whose addiction to city jungle methods demands much stronger measures of control. Again you go back to the group (in terms of relations power, the group is your shepherd, you shall not want). Level with them; tell them exactly what, with their cooperation, you intend to do. You might open this part of the discussion by saying, "You have to help me control your thugs. There is nothing that I as a single person can do to stop them, since I can't be everywhere at once. But there is plenty that you as their victims can do. For one thing, there are many more of you than there are of them. Does anybody have any suggestions?" Misreading your intent, someone may pipe up, "Gang up on 'em and beat hell out of 'em!" As appealing as this may sound—and the bullies deserve it—you turn it down. "That isn't the best way. In fact, someone may get seriously injured, and that's the last thing we want. Anybody got a better idea?"

"You beat them up!"

"I'm not allowed to." You don't add that you *could* lose such a fight, which would *really* leave them in a fix.

What are you waiting for them to say? Just this. You are waiting for the tenor of their suggestions to change from violent means of handling an aggressor to nonviolent techniques. When that moment comes, you've taken them another mile in their slow march toward self-government. I was pleasantly surprised during one such meeting when one of my boys said the magic words.

"Ostracize him!" The speaker was a frail, bespectacled lad whose parents were Black Muslims.

"Ostracize him? What do you mean by that?" I knew damn well what he meant; I wanted to be sure that the rest of the group knew.

"Well, don't none of us talk to him or listen to him or lend him things or pal around with him." The other boys nodded in quick agreement.

"Exactly! There's just one hooker in this, though. What's the only way you can make this ostracism work?"

"Everybody has to do it," another boy answered.

"Right! Now does everybody here think that he can do it? I mean, once we have identified the person who keeps this dorm in an uproar, are you willing to apply this pressure for as long as it takes?"

"Yes!" Now it is time to name names. Let them do the naming, not you, for it might be someone you didn't suspect. If ever you want to see a thug wilt, to grow smaller before your eyes, watch one of them try to squirm out of that cage he sees his former prey erecting around him. Don't, for once he breaks this wall of silence without having to reform, you'll lose him and the group—forever. Of course, the door is kept open for him to re-enter the fold once he mends his ways. Make sure that he has mended them, though.

Make sure that the aggressor apologizes—every time—for two reasons. It is a good social and personal trait to develop, and the embarrassment of having to eat a little crow in front of the group is a strong deterrent to repeating the act, psychotics and psychopaths excused. Don't say, "I want you to apologize." Rather, make sure in conversation that he admits to being wrong, that he knows he was wrong. Then ask, "Don't you think it would be nice to apologize to Herkimer?"—or Asdrubal or whoever the injured party was.

I excuse psychopaths and psychotics because they can rarely accept responsibility for their acts. It is always someone else's fault. Or they will deny that it ever occurred at all. The denial will be vigorous, sustained, and hostile; and they aren't lying, because in this confabulation (invention of false memory or denial of a real one) they are light-years away from reality. To them, *you* are a little screwy. I remember seeing one such boy whom I had been writing reports to my supervisor about for weeks slap another youngster in the head, and reply seconds later to my remonstrance that he did not do it. The kid actually had tears in his eyes in his sincerity. He had earlier bopped a counselor in the head with a shoe and given her the same routine. I had to bypass my sleeping supervisor to have him handled.

Does ostracism work with every bully? No, but it does with ninety per cent of them (in my experience), and a 90 per cent return on any investment is the best game in town. Once you have brought this level of organization and cooperation into your group, they will begin to behave with more social responsibility than the public at large. Item: How many neighborhoods can you think of where the people banded together and successfully froze out the hoods? Congratulations.

A word of caution. The foregoing method should be necessary only once during the residency of a particular company of boys. The reason is that this is rather powerful medicine and applying it two or three times as often will not lead to two or three times the benefits that you get from one dose. Besides, I've never seen a bully come back for a second shot anyway, with the exception of those who had other symptoms that led me to believe that they were psychotic or extremely immature.

A psychological diagnosis should only be made by your professional staff, but there are hints and clues that you can watch out for that should put you on guard. For example, the psychopath is completely indifferent to whether something that he has done is right or wrong, or whether it was injurious to someone else. You can sometimes derive this information by close questioning and sharp observation of him. On the other hand, some such individuals are quite expert at conning the unwary counselor with "right" answers to questions that are aimed at discovering what makes him tick. To hear him tell it, he wants only to do what's right, since his being locked up was all a big mistake anyhow. In some children's institutions, data on these emotional deviants is placed in their files long before they get to the dorm, so the wise counselor would do well to read all the folders that are made available to him. A case episode will better illustrate how a certain amount of nosiness can save you a barrel of trouble.

In an Ohio diagnostic center, I arrived one night to find a new youngster, whom I'll call Lee, entered on the roster. He was sixteen and a refugee from Cleveland's Hough Avenue hell. I took no further notice of the record than its description of him as a large black boy who chewed toothpicks and kept to himself. Shortly after the boys were awakened the next morning, I heard loud screaming from the kitchen area where the breakfast crew was dispensing the food. When I rushed in, there was this new fellow, a tall, glowering kid, choking one of the kitchen boys and screaming at the top of his voice for a second helping of Frosty Flakes. In the office, the only defense he had for his actions was that he had seen some of the other boys with two boxes of cereal and we had damned well better not hold out on him. That he had endangered another's life for a box of flakes seemed to have little or no importance for him; he was simply not going to be denied what was rightly his. Of course, fighting over trifles is not unusual for people behind locked doors, as you know, but something in the fierceness of Lee's assault, the cold hatred in his face, moved me to read his folder more carefully.

According to the center's psychologist, Lee was one in whom violence was a barely controlled part of his make-up; that is, it was a wellspring of energy that he was likely to dip into at any time for a real or imagined offense. The psychologist underlined in his report that the counselor was at no time to turn his back on the boy, for he seemed to lack the inhibiting fears or self-preservative functions that regulate the behavior of most of the rest of us. In plain language, he'd bash your head in for a stick of gum, regardless of who you were. I wrote this warning in large letters and underlined it in red pencil on the daily calendar for the day crew.

The psychopath requires long-term professional counseling, with a poor prognosis. My wager is that such service is not available at your plant. So you keep dropping him into your supervisor's lap to make sure that he stays as aware of it as you are and so that he can't pretend surprise when one of your little boys comes up with fractured ribs or a broken arm, courtesy of someone like Lee.

A further word about the reading of the boys' records. Some institutions forbid it for fear that a vindictive counselor might use it against the youngsters. For instance, suppose a boy has a history of sexual abuse on smaller children and has been trying to reform and live down his past. Then one day he has a disagreement with his counselor over some house procedure or interpretation of the rules and *wins* his point. It is conceivable that if said counselor is a small-minded man, he might humiliate the boy in front of his peers with a dramatic disclosure of this privileged information. The question of how much a counselor should know about his youngsters' pasts is still a controversial one.

My feeling is that the advantages of the counselor knowing exactly what he is dealing with far outweigh the potential embarrassments to the boys from having their files read. It should be house policy that any counselor who abuses his authority in order to bring disgrace on a kid in the way described above (or any similar way) is subject to summary dismissal. This weeds out the nitwits. In the section dealing with failures in individual management, I discuss at length a case episode in which a boy who had made the rounds of several mental institutions was dropped into our dorm without our being told anything of his history of emotional upset. It was a real circus until we found out.

If your institution allows you to examine the records, it is extremely important that you qualify what is said about them according to the various people reporting. In other words, if such and such is the opinion of the social worker or of the teacher, it should be so designated in the file. If you cannot make out where the psychologist's findings leave off and the other professionals' observations begin, you should take the time and effort to find out. Here's why.

Everybody who puts something into a boy's file has a definite reason for putting it there, which differs somewhat from whatever caused the next person or the preceding person to write. In other words, a schoolteacher may be impressed by a youngster's learning ability or lack of it, while a nurse may be concerned about his need for better hygiene, neither of which may be related to the appearance of aggressiveness that the psychologist remarks on, and so forth. While it is obvious that anyone who feels moved to comment on the boy should state in his report his name, title, the circumstances under which the situation developed and, in fact, use a special form provided for his department, this is a frequently neglected formality in many homes. An unsigned, unnotated opinion is of extremely limited value; it's like an anonymous letter.

There are other reasons for treading cautiously through a boy's folder. Not only do reasons differ, but there is a wide range of competencies among the people making the entries. When two observers make conflicting statements about the same kid, there are three possible truths. They could both be right, neither could be right, or only one might be. And if the difference is important, like that between a straight boy and a budding thief, or between a chronic liar and one who confabulates, the new counselor should withhold his own decision until he knows something about the other observers. He has to keep in mind that a boy can be Little Lord Fauntleroy with him but Mr. Hyde when he steps out the door.

This was really brought home to me a number of years back by a lad in a children's institution in Ohio. He was black, a fourth grader, bright, helpful in the dorm, always said sir, please, and thank you. His general behavior had more lace in it than Liberace's collar. On the first day that he was scheduled to go to school, I got him ready, sent him out and promptly forgot him. About thirty minutes later the phone rang; the assistant principal was on the other end. To make a long story short, Little Lord Fauntleroy had spent his first moments in school running his hand up the teacher's dress. The first time he did it, she had demanded that he come out into the hall. This pleased hell out of him, because now there was no one to watch him and giggle as his classmates had been doing. He went to town, as the saying goes, while she was trying to bawl him out. When they reached the principal's office, the dumbfounded schoolmarm holding him at arm's length and battling his grasping fingers, he started in on the assistant principal, who, it doesn't need to be pointed out, was also a woman.

There were three interesting sidelights to this little episode. One was that no one could decide whether the little character needed a psychiatrist, a stern talking to, a walloping, or all three. The second was that all his male counselors and advisers had been praising him to the stars, for with us he was a gem. The third was that neither woman was as angry with him as I'd seen them on other occasions with boys who had swiped someone's eraser or shown up late for class.

The major point, though, is that your boys are often inconsistent in behavior. This is something to keep under your wig when the reports don't dovetail.

For a number of reasons, grown-ups are also guilty of inconsistencies. One of these reasons is racism. Having a university education doesn't exempt us from the very American habit of putting the worst possible construction on the motives of the "others." We're still kind of benighted about skin shades. One case history will do for this well-worn topic.

Two boys, one black and one white, were buddies in an Ohio detention home. They were fifteen. They slept together, played pool together, ate together, shoved the other boys out of the way so that they could stand in dinner line together. They even tried one night to go AWOL together. In short, real good friends. Their one problem in the dorm was that they were bullies; not particular vicious ones, but they did take liberties with the rest of the group. Outwardly, the aggression they showed was equal and we made note of it in their records, for they were an inseparable pair, even in "bogarting." However, they were interviewed separately by a white social worker and a white psychologist, who were to confer together and recommend placement for the boys. The upshot of all this was that the white youngster was sent to an honor camp, the black to the horrors of an "industrial school." When I looked into the professional résumés in their folders, I discovered that the white kid's antics were viewed as mere high-spiritedness, while they considered the black to be a budding menace to society. And that's the way it turned out, because he really learned the tricks of the underground trade from the hoodlums he had for company in the "industrial school."

Is error on the negative side the only way that racism can screw up a kid's future? Nope. When a social worker has the American sickness and feels guilty about it, the more common form this guilt or anxiety about anti-black bias takes is an oversolicitude in the treatment of the youngster. In other words, for the social worker a black child can do no wrong. He could have been seen standing over a bleeding robbery victim with a dripping knife in his hand and the guilt-ridden social worker or counselor will make the assault seem like something heroic when he or she gets through explaining it away. The psychologists have a fancy name for this kind of behavior: reaction formation. By refusing to find any fault with black youths, they defend themselves against—and, they think, conceal from others—the anxiety that their prejudice arouses. The worst result of it is that the youth himself is harmed, rather than helped, by this "favoritism." It is one thing to have insight into the creation of a black youth's self-destructive behavior by the social injustices that have been heaped upon the black population; it is quite another to imply condonement of acts that result in his incarceration and separation from his family. The ultimate outcome is further personal disablement *added onto* the political burdens of being black.

I was hit between the eyes by just such a situation one

Sunday morning when two boys, one black and one Puerto Rican, whom we had allowed out on pass were brought back to the institution by city police. They had been arrested on suspicion of using narcotics. According to the cops, they were inhaling from a brown paper bag and behaving as though they had a "high." I was in the office when the boys were brought in. I heard their story and observed them. Indeed they did look droopy-eyed. They kept begging me to let them lie down and rest; this was only three hours after they had got up, so I knew what the score was. I was about to have them sent over to the hospital for a medical examination (which they refused) when their social worker, a white girl from an eastern school, dashed in, listened to their version of what had happened, discounted the police report entirely, suggested that I do the same, and wondered aloud why I was so reluctant to let them lie down instead of talking about a doctor. My reason was simply that if they were ill or "high," it was the center's responsibility to care for them. In addition, I wasn't buying what they were selling, which was: they just happened to see this innocent-looking bag lying in the park, a park that is littered with thousands of identical bags, picked it up to see what was inside, became so curious that they had to smell what was inside, when these two mean old cops came up and collared them.

I didn't get my medical check-up, they didn't get their bed rest, she didn't get her anxiety relieved. The poor girl's parting shot was that something should be done about getting the boys a nap in the daytime. I agreed in principle, but not for the purpose of sleeping off a high. The end of it all? A few weeks later the Puerto Rican was discovered to be a junkie; the black boy's parents complained to the authorities that we were too lax in keeping their son from access to drugs and demanded that he be removed from our too-trusting hands. They threatened to sue us for not finding him out sooner.

8. OTHER BENEFITS

The benefits to be gained from group meetings go far

beyond the limits of gaining group control, although this was its immediate purpose. Depending on the way they are conducted, the meetings can drop a lot of other bonuses into the counselor's lap. In the preceding pages, most of what I had to say concerned the solution of problems, and in this setting the counselor did most of the talking. In point of fact, once dormitory peace has been secured, the counselor should be able to move into the background at these get-togethers while the boys conduct the proceedings. Now this requires a certain amount of formal organization within the sessions, with certain boys delegated to handle the responsibilities of leadership, order, agenda, and record-keeping. Few accomplishments are as pleasing as seeing a group of youngsters officially labeled as "losers," delinquents, antisocial, and so forth, carrying on a dormitory meeting, employing parliamentary rules and democratic procedures, listening to each other, respecting each other, the whole works. It is particularly great if this is the same bunch who were formerly hard-knuckled, alienated hell-raisers. If you haven't seen a transformation like this, man, you haven't lived.

Meetings are for communication, getting to know one another. It was in a group meeting that they met you (the "new" you if this is an old group with whom you formerly did not have group sessions). They should be held daily, preferably during the day shift (8:00 a.m.—4:00 p.m.). However, if school or work schedules prevent a number of boys from being present, then an afternoon time will have to do. Whichever time is chosen, the meetings should be held at approximately the same hour each day, even though the length of the sessions may vary. This reduces the occasions for the boys' "forgetting" when the sessions are to begin.

Second, most of the talking should be done by the boys after the initial purpose of control has been gained. The reason is that the setting of rules for dormitory, dining-room, and playground behavior must pass to their hands if they are ever to grow. It is *their* ideas and problems that are to be aired. How soon this transfer takes place depends, of course, on their readiness for it. With one group it may happen within a couple of days; with another it may take weeks before they can carry it off without the counselor running the show. My feeling is, the sooner you can turn it over to them, the better. If you have a group of peewees, that is, boys from seven to ten, then of course you will have to do most or all of the conducting. With older boys you should be able to take a minor role, say, sergeant-at-arms or doorman.

It is not my purpose to be too specific in the mechanics of these dormitory sessions, but there is one hard and fast rule that seems to help most in the development of the group process. That rule is: only one person may talk at a time and he must signal his desire to talk by raising his hand. As for the rest of it, you and the boys can settle on your own style. There may be a tendency among some groups to choose or elect a dormitory leader or president. Sometimes it works out fine, but my personal bias is against selecting a big wheel. It puts a lot of pressure on the youngster to walk a chalk line; he may feel that he has some "authority," which others may resent. Worse, he may expect some special favors from the counselor that the fair-minded counselor cannot grant. Finally, should he become moody or "go sour," it may set back the growth of others who have been identifying with him. How the boy who chairs the meeting is selected is up to you and the group, but you avoid trouble and spread the sense of involvement around if this is a rotating chairmanship that changes, say, once a week.

Group meetings are an excellent means of orienting new arrivals in the dorm. They step into a calm society where individual expression is respected. This is reassuring to most of them. (But not all. See "Dee" in Book II.) It also saves the counselor from having to go through the introductory waltz every time a new face appears.

Unfortunately it sometimes happens that a counselor will use these meetings to harangue the boys or to peddle his personal politics. I recall one such fellow whose hang-up was the color of God and the origin of man. It so happened that the race of which the boys were members had a color opposite to that which he was ascribing to

God and Adam. Needless to say, he didn't get very far with his group on any level.

Book II
The Counselor and The Individual

1. THE THIRD FLOOR

The rest of this message concerns itself with your relationship to the boys on a one-to-one basis and is predicated on group control having first been established. The boys have set up their dormitory government, and a functional society now exists that inhibits anti-social acts and encourages self-realizing, constructive behavior. In other words, we are about to attempt to haul Al's elevator up to the third floor. We have made our control-level stop and have bidden it what we hope will be a permanent farewell. It wasn't a bad department, just unspirited and uninspiring. In the back of our minds, though, we acknowledge how essential it was.

Please, a redefinition. In "Taking Hold," I defined the counselor as a salesman, the advocate of a new life style. Since we are now talking about your youngsters as individuals, it is necessary to extend that notion of the counselor's role to another, perhaps startling, level. Because not only are you pushing them toward new avenues of expression; not only are you selling them new language, new habits of projecting into the future (planning); not only are you instilling in them a new regard for other people and their parents and themselves, but you yourself are part of the merchandise, daddy-o. Here's why.

As boys grow up, one of the most important determinants of the eventual role they choose for themselves in life is the available male model. This taking on of some of the characteristics of an admired older person is called identification. Now I have already explained and it has been demonstrated conclusively that most of our delinquent boys, particularly black boys, come from homes in which there was a physically or emotionally remote father. This creates for most of them an insurmountable problem in sociability. Put in plainer language, the question "Who am I?" is never answered in a socially acceptable way, which is to say, in a way that will lead a youth to the completion of high school, toward training for a vocation or a profession. There is no man in the home, working, bringing home the bacon, helping mom raise the kids, so why in hell should he gear himself to do it? As a matter of fact, this masculine absence and the presence of an authoritative, domineering (out of necessity) female parent has led many boys into the confused role assumption of the homosexual.

There was a time when this problem of identity was somewhat eased by schoolmasters who were long on understanding and dedication to their jobs, and by ministers. But school is much less personal now, more crowded, and staffed by younger teachers looking forward only to the deliverance of quitting time. I can remember my high school principal of a generation back, a kindly, stern, Latin-quoting father figure who used to haunt the alleys and sidestreets around the school, looking for class-cutters and budding delinquents. His voice was like the martial roll of drums and his disapproving frown could cow a Dunbar truant back into regular attendance. Because of his influence, for a long time I harbored the notion of becoming a principal; I even wanted a paunch like his. Of course, the secret of his tremendous power over us was the obvious fact that he gave a damn. Not that he ever said so. He didn't have to. It showed in his despair over some of our more horrendous acts, like smoking reefers, cutting classes, cutting each other. They don't make educators like that by the gross ton.

In the absence of other models in the home or school whose emulation or influence could be constructive in their lives, your boys did the natural thing. They took what was available, which was to adopt the code for behavior as laid down by their ghetto peers and the wolves of their neighborhood—and wound up being relegated to your care. Now the longer the time a boy has had to soak up these self-destructive values, the more deeply imbedded they are in his pattern of behavior; or the longer he had to do without the aid and guidance of a father—and this is usually for most of his boyhood—the more susceptible he was to the seductions of the street. Age therefore becomes a factor that limits the amount of success you can expect when you encounter a group of older boys. Basing it entirely on experience and observation over the past seventeen years, I would say that the age thirteen to fourteen appears to be particularly crucial. Up to that time the counselor's chances of putting himself over as a credible identification model are far better than with boys in the fifteen to seventeen age range. *Don't be misled* by all this, because here I am generalizing in order to temper your great expectations with reality. And as with all generalizations, the exceptions are legion. You cannot apply blanket rules to individuals. They apply and are intended to apply only to groups in terms of expected percentages of success and failure. So never write off a particular youngster because he has passed his fifteenth or sixteenth birthday.

In applying the Relations Method to guidance of the individual, the counselor has to keep alert to the quality of the interaction between himself and the boy. This demands a high level of sensitiveness on the part of the group leader, for it is in his power—in fact, it is his responsibility—to set the tone of this interaction. Something must first come across from you to the boy, something human, something personal, something constructive; and he will reply in God knows what kind of way. This something must be the fact that you give a damn about him, that you could care less about what he's done (though you should know as part of your data about him), that what you want to do is help him ready himself for a future that he can enjoy in freedom, pride, and happiness. I know this sounds like preachifying, but I've never seen anything less than this work. Why?

When you demonstrate by your attitude and actions that you are sincerely concerned for his welfare, you are in a psychological way extending your hand to this youngster. The closest physical parallel is the reach of a lifeguard to a floundering swimmer, and like the life-saving operation, this proffered help, this glimpse you give him of your essential humanity and your willingness to become involved in the reconstitution of his personality and of his life, carries within it the potential for either a successful rescue or a mutual drowning. Many a lifeguard has been pulled to the bottom by a panicked swimmer and has had to abandon the struggle in order to save himself. Still, rescues do occur; the beaches are always jammed; life and the quest continue. Your boys, injured through the vicissitudes of survival in the asphalt jungle to disappointment, to betrayal, to mendacity, to—in a word—the everlasting *phoniness* of the adult world, may not at first respond to your proffered hand. Some may, in fact, spit on it, which is to say, answer you with suspicion and hostility. This is a frequent consequence with older boys. After all, if their real parents loved them not, what should they expect from you, a paid stranger whose predecessors may have slopped them like hogs, flung ill-fitting clothing at them and barely tolerated them until the deliverance of quitting time? Nothing at all, their instinct warns them.

There is, of course, an additional underlying reason for their enduring reluctance to meet you halfway, and this is particularly significant in the origin of the older boys' hostility. Given the absence of any real psychopathology, they are *afraid* to react humanly to, develop a dependency on, or even to like, a counselor. They once loved their parents or an uncle or an aunt and where the hell did that get them? So when you reach out your hand and grope for an answering clasp from him, you are trying to breach a wall that the gnarled hand of adult indifference has had years to erect and to reinforce. Therefore, never be surprised or dismayed when you feel in his attitude only cold masonry, the hardness of mortared cynicism.

It is good to know, however, that you will win a far greater number of times than you will lose, and, of course, the younger the boy, the better are your chances. In one case that I can recall, my success in getting through to a refugee, that is, calling forth from him a normal affective response, produced a rather poignant side effect. A twelve-year-old Puerto Rican child named Cesar who had been remanded to our care through a child-abuse petition had been in our dorm for two or three weeks. In that time he had adjusted fairly well to group living and was generally a well-behaved boy. He seemed to think rather highly of me as an adult who could be trusted and with whom he could relax. For a youngster coming from a family background of neglect from mother and beatings from father severe enough to warrant court removal from their jurisdiction, this was one hell of a milestone. Anyway, one day I walked in, and a kid from another dorm with whom I was friendly rushed up and hugged me around the waist. That was a mistake. I heard Cesar yell, "Let go my counselor, you punk!" and the battle was on. The moral? Jealousy is very much a part of the "normal affective response," and the alert counselor would do well to look out for it. Cesar simply figured that I "belonged" to him.

What goes on in the Relations relationship? What is it exactly? In this relationship the counselor does three things: 1) he digs up worms; 2) he goes fishing; 3) he hauls in his catch.

Worm-digging is what a bird does to feed its young. The relations counselor makes sure that the practical needs of the dormitory and the boys are taken care of. He scrounges up, for example, enough clothes, toothbrushes, soap, brooms, mattresses, blankets, pillows, towels from the supply room or wherever they are supposed to come from. Sometimes these articles are hard to get. They usually are if the counselor merely submits a form to his supervisor and waits for the goods to come raining down on him. For some reason, there is nothing quite so easy to get lost, misplaced, or sidetracked as a written request for dormitory supplies. In my experience the counselor usually has to make follow-up inquiry to get his goods (if your institution operates smoothly in this respect, it is an exception). When other people tell you you are making a nuisance of yourself, you're probably showing about the right amount of diligence. Keep pushing till they come across down in the stockroom. So frustrating is it to be told repeatedly that they are out of T shirts, towels, et cetera, or that the new supplies haven't arrived yet, that I have been tempted to raid other, better-stocked dormitories to get things for mine. Being driven to this extreme helps you to understand better why the boys are motivated to steal.

I don't need to tell you how the boys react to the one man who does the worm-digging, especially if he's the only guy on his shift who seems to have "his shit together," as the saying goes. It is a tangible sign that you are embattled for them, even though it may not, strictly speaking, be your job to do the hunting. And if you are the only hustler (heaven forbid), it isn't long before the kids start meeting you at the door, telling you what they've run out of. Which is usually everything every day.

You now take your worms and go fishing. At proper times during the day, you talk to your youngsters about items of general interest. As individuals they are interested in different things, and different ones will hook up with different things that you say. But why should they listen to you in the first place? A good reason, but not the only one, is that by now you have shown your involvement by taking pains to secure their practical needs, the needs of any human being, in an institution or outside of it.

The topic they are most interested in is themselves. This isn't the only thing, of course, but it will do for openers. These "relations" talks may occur within your group meetings or at other times. I would avoid them at the group sessions, because then the boys are supposed to be doing the talking, working on their dorm problems. The time I would usually use was when the boys were settling down for bed. Another good time is when you're dispensing evening snacks. The tone of this talk is conversational, somewhat lighthearted, but about something serious. Whenever it is done, the dorm atmosphere should be relaxed and free of tension.

What I usually open with with a new group is what boyhood seems to be all about, what purpose there is in taking so long to grow up. I speak of boyhood as being a rehearsal for manhood, and of the effects that the habits they form in boyhood will have on the kind of men they will be. For some reason, this subject is a winner with boys in the thirteen to seventeen age range.

Another winner is their future responsibility as fathers. I was surprised to find this square subject to be so well received. The night I brought it up, I half expected to be yawned out of the room, for many of my boys claimed to hate their fathers. Why in hell should they care about becoming better fathers? They did. At one time the group agitator, the kind of guy who gets two other people to fight while he stands on the sidelines, wanted to discuss the same thing night after night: what a father should do for his children.

Of course, a big topic of interest is girls. One of my biggest gripes is the counselor who passes himself off as a Romeo and whose professed method of relating to women is sex exploitation. Right on for him if he can stand himself, but boys need to know that there are many other things in the boy-girl relationship and that if they look no further into it than the prospect of sex, they will miss most of what our sex and personality differences are all about. I recall one counselor whose theme on the subject was various ways to screw . . . . and that was all.

Another subject of vital interest is drugs. The counselor would do well to become very well informed on it. My approach to it was economical rather than moral (morality is a hell of a hard thing to try to teach). I found that they were very interested in the economics of the drug transaction, that is, who was benefiting and who was the chump. With black boys I read page 191 of *The Godfather* to let them know what the Mafia thinks of them as a race of people and as drug users.

Future jobs are another extremely interesting and vital subject, though I feel a little shaky talking about it. The reason is the recession that blacks have been in since 1929 and whites for the past three years (with a few glimpses of daylight). That the recession of 1971 was contrived through governmental action ("Let's fight inflation through an increase in unemployment") does not make it more palatable to the man whose job is sacrificed. And I have yet to hear an Administration spokesman who was willing to give up *his* job as a sign of his commitment to this noble purpose. But an even worse kind of planned unemployment is that based on the race of the job-seeker. One of the most infuriating spectacles I have ever seen is that of the lily-white construction gangs working on high-risers in Manhattan and Buffalo and Columbus, their union ranks kept "full" by advertising in Europe and Canada for workers to come to bountiful America, while a few blocks away black men and Puerto Rican men languish on streetcorners, their sons roaming the streets (or in our centers) and their wives accepting welfare.

It is a damnable irony that these selfsame construction-union members are the loudest critics of the welfare system, claiming that it destroys men's initiative to work. Their union policies (which include advocating a four-day work week) have done more to destroy "initiative" than those anemic assistance checks, which are, in fact, necessitated by those selfsame policies. The workers in downtown Manhattan justify their racism with the statement, "We built this union up and we're going to keep it!" I have to admire men who have the gall to talk like that (and it *does* take gall . . . or ignorance), particularly since many, perhaps most, of them are first-generation Americans whose immigrant parents have yet to learn to speak English. I have heard militants suggest that instead of promoting personality development, schoolteachers and child-care workers among the Third World children should teach proper handling of dynamite caps and fuses and the fashioning of Molotov cocktails. Whatever the merits of this argument (and they may be considerable), it occurs to me that no matter who runs the world our boys step back into and no matter what style of government and system of economics prevail, the same kinds of personality traits will be in demand. Dependability, punctuality, self-respect, and respect for others are as highly prized in black communities as in white, and as essential in socialist systems as in capitalist, fascist, or communist. It takes the same kind of aggressiveness, self-discipline, foresight, elbowing and persistence to get ahead in one as in any other. It would be extremely interesting to compare the personality profiles of the heads of Western European (socialist) countries with those of the Communist Party leadership and of the board of directors of Ford Motor Company. How different, really, would they be?

Whatever your subject, I find that the boys will listen if *you* will listen. I have heard one counselor screw up the dialogue by turning it into a put-down, telling them how smart he was and how much more he had than they. This same counselor later was observed borrowing money and records from the boys. They got a big laugh out of it.

Why is this known as "fishing"? Because the boys are listening and watching and weighing you, what you have to say, and particularly the way you act. Some of them will be able to relate to (become hooked by) your style and some will not. It's hard to predict who or how many. One thing that turns a lot of them off is the guy in the relations dialogue who sounds like he's preaching. They've heard preachers before. A dialogue is an exchange. The individuals who adopt your style and some of your attitudes are your "catch."

Now how does the counselor decide which boy or boys need individual attention? Suppose there are five or six out of the population who seem in need of it. What does the hard-pressed counselor do? While these are very common dilemmas, there are no ready-made answers to them. However, as a general rule, the counselor should concern himself in particular with that youngster for whom the group relationship seems not to allow enough security, opportunities for expression, or feeling of growth (achievement). Let's put it another way. A boy who needs you somewhat more than the rest will signal you by being outstanding (sometimes painfully so) in some way, such as being depressed, a bully, apathetic, a thief, a school truant, loud—you name it. The key word here is need, as opposed to want. I recall one Puerto Rican boy who was so lonely and depressed that for days he refused to eat and refused to listen to our pleas that he eat. Of course, this is an extreme example. In most cases, the best approach is for you to set a reproducible example.

With this Relations Method (really, adult behavior modeling), how can you tell whether you are getting through to a boy? Are there any reliable signs that will tell you when you are on target? One answer is that you may never know except by retrospect, that is, by bumping into him years later and discovering how it all turned out. On the other hand, there are dozens of little ways that they as human beings may communicate to you quite unconsciously that something in your presentation of yourself and of your program has awakened an answering humanity in them. In some cases it will occur in boys to whom you paid no special attention. This is a bonus of the Relations Method. Your boys are not so sophisticated that a fondness for and an identification with a counselor can be hidden very long, despite a desire to conceal it beneath a layer of hostility or worldliness. One small sign: I once had a favorite expression that I used when I wanted to criticize something, like a poorly made bed. I'd look at it, turn my mouth down at the corners and mumble, *"That's* rich. That's *real* rich." A tough Dayton sixteen-year-old who had been with us for a couple of weeks and had always cursed when something displeased him soon began to say instead, *"That's* rich. That's *real* rich." A small thing, but this is an important sign of assimilation, that is, absorbing someone else's style. He eventually dropped the tough stance and became a well-adjusted youngster.

In a group that I managed some months ago, I noticed that one young fellow, with whom I had had no particular rapport, always stood very close to me whenever we rode the elevator to the dining hall and always managed to walk next to me whenever we went hiking or on an entertainment trip downtown. He had very little to say; he just glued himself as closely to me as he could. With the passage of time he began to ask questions about my schooling, my background, children, ambitions, hobbies, personal likes and dislikes, and so on. I answered him candidly and good-naturedly. Outside of these question-and-answer periods he said little, following group routines quietly. Eventually the time came when I had to explain to the boys that I had to resign the job to pursue my studies at Columbia, and under the terms of my fellowship I would not be allowed to work here any longer. The young fellow took this very hard. He complained that the school was dirty to put this kind of restriction on me and suggested that he and some of the other youngsters would get outside jobs to pay my way through school so that I wouldn't have to follow Columbia's dictates at all. And could keep working there.

One of the disadvantages of the Relations Method is that the counselor runs the risk of breaking some kid's heart. This is one basis of my belief that child counseling should be elevated into a lifelong profession, like school-teaching or dentistry. The kids grow up before you bug out.

I went through the above episodes to answer the question of how you can tell when they are taking hold. A boy who despises you or is indifferent to you will make no effort to associate himself with you at all and will have no interest in your living style whatsoever. When a child asks you questions about yourself, he is doing what you do when you walk into a clothing store. He's trying on your experiences, your personality, your coping methods for size. This imposes a big responsibility on the counselor. If you fit, that is, if he sees in what you tell him some chance that he, by following the same or a similar path, can survive at least as well as you have, then this first outward reach for identification will be a successful one. This is therefore an important crossroads that the two of you have reached. Don't blow it. Don't be a smart-ass. Would you believe that I have heard some counselors who had made it this far with a youngster claim that they got to their present position by making clever decisions at every crucial point in their lives? You place an intolerable burden on the youngster with this kind of horse manure, for he knows that he isn't superhuman or superclever (though he may not know that you aren't either). Given answers like "I was always a good student and used to pick daisies for the principal's desk," or "I was the 1969 winner of the Young Man Most

Likely ... award at my [suburban] high school," his attempt to identify is crushed before it ever gets off the ground. No, this doesn't mean that you should put yourself down if you did happen to be a daisy-picker; nothing wrong with that, or with YMMLTS. But it's better to try to find some common point of reference, like my family was big like yours ... or, I wasn't too crazy about school myself until ... or, I used to think it was great to hang out all night too until ... or, the idea of smoking (pot) was real exciting until. ... The untils are important because you are trying to lead him to some point of new beginning. Of course, if you can't truthfully say any of this and really can't find any common ground, simply be yourself. Provided that you are a "together" guy, it's usually enough.

A good question at this point is whether there are people who, regardless of their level of training and techniques, will never be able to put themselves over with the youngsters. Yes. The best criterion is whether you are able in your own mind to separate the boy from his antisocial acts or crime. This may be one hell of a difficult thing to do, which is why good counselors are in such short supply. A number of well-meaning people think that this means to accept everything the youngster does with a weak-kneed compliance. Not by a long shot. A handy rule of thumb is to praise or compliment when they do something constructive and self-improving and to show strong disapproval when they do something destructive of themselves or others, making sure that they understand the reason for your reaction. Within this rule, however, there is a whole universe of considerations and compromises, sensitivities and shades of gray, a universe within which you and a youngster can maneuver and search and perhaps find the right formula for his re-creation.

The episode that I had with "Jonah" is told to you because it has some elements of success and failure. No approach to child guidance is perfect, and were I to omit or gloss over my errors, you would have rightly put me down for a visionary or phony. I also think that you can learn almost as much from making miscues as from succeeding. After all, if you stub your toe in the dark, at least you know where not to place your big foot next time. By lumping these bruises together, I hope to drive home a lesson or two.

The case history of "Kewpie" is given to illustrate how the typical bureaucratic elephant in a boys' home often tramples counselors and boys alike in its stately march to that graveyard called "proper procedure."

In terms of depth of personality damage, "Dee" was the most bruised boy that I have ever worked with. Like most of what goes on in your work with boys, the case history of "Dee" is another mixture of success and failure.

And finally we come to the case history of "Vio" The Magnificent. It represents a success story of the Relations Method at its best, that is, when the counselor takes care of all the practical tasks that he is capable of and at the same time has enough energy and commitment left to give that extra minute to pause and listen, and go to bat for a battling youngster on whom the institution had given up. Putting it last also allows me to end on a high note. I'd rather go out smiling than with a mouth full of sand.

2

"JONAH"

Jonah was a thirteen-year-old black child who was brought into the children's home in a large northeastern city on a PINS petition (person in need of supervision). He arrived on a day when I was off, so I knew nothing of his first reaction to the group. He first came to my attention by way of complaining that someone had stolen some cologne from his locker. I looked up from my desk at a tall (for his age), rather slender, light-complexioned youth who was somewhat mature-looking. His manner was watchful, yet respectful.

"What kind of cologne was it?" I asked.

"Aqua Velva. I had just bought it."

"So the bottle was full."

"Yes."

"How many guys knew you had it?"

"I don't know. I didn't try to keep it any kind of secret. I didn't think anyone would bother it if I kept it in my locker."

"Was there a lock on your locker?"

"No."

"Well, you might as well know now that if there's no lock on the door, things will just seem to walk right out of your locker."

At this time there were fifteen boys in the dorm. Five were Puerto Rican, the rest were black. When the word spread that Jonah's toilet water was missing, one of the black kids, a boy called Deke, immediately offered his help in finding the culprit and the missing cologne. In fact, he claimed that he already knew who had stolen it.

"It was one of the reekans!" he exclaimed at the next group meeting.

"What's a reekan?" I asked.

"Puerto Rican ... a greaser!" he replied, grinning broadly. Deke was also thirteen, though at that time he was claiming to be fifteen. He was a recent transfer from the city Youth House, where boys who have been adjudged delinquent are housed, which in terms of street values carried more prestige than merely being picked up for school truancy or incorrigibility at home. Deke wore his Youth House background proudly. He was a rather handsome, very dark-skinned youngster. The Puerto Rican boys stirred rather uneasily at his characterization of them, but said nothing.

"Let's cut out the reekan or greaser bit," I said a little angrily. "Just tell us how you know that one of them took it."

"Because I saw him!"

"Oh? Okay, who was it?"

"It was him," he answered, pointing at one of the Latin boys, a kid named Manuel, who was so startled that he fell backward in his chair. Deke was still grinning delightedly. All the black boys glared at Manuel; the Puerto Ricans merely stared down at their shoes. All except Manuel.

"Me?" he exclaimed, jumping up. "You crazy or something? I never took nothing out of nobody's locker!"

"You lie!" Deke shot back. "I saw you take it yesterday morning when everyone was lining up for breakfast."

"Why didn't you say something about it then to me or to Jonah?" I asked.

"I thought he'd put it back, like borrowing it or something. Besides, I like to mind my own business."

A word about Manuel. Unfortunately he had already been discovered in the act of taking someone else's belongings and he did, in fact, have the reputation of being a liar. So Deke had chosen fertile ground to plant suspicion.

"Now what we ought to do," Deke went on, speaking more to the black boys than to me, "is search this reekan's locker, and if we don't find the bottle there, go through the rest of *their*—" he nodded his head at the Latin youngsters—"dressers. Then if we still don't find it, we ought to kick some tail till we do!"

I held my fire. I wanted to see just how far he would get with this call for black racism. In the sullen quiet, the Puerto Rican boys began to shift in their chairs; a defiant look was hardening their expressions. The black boys waited, saying nothing. They were awaiting a sign from Jonah, the aggrieved party. If he wanted to hassle the other boys for his cologne, the blacks, it was plain, were at his disposal with plenty of muscle power. Of course, the longer Jonah waited, the shorter the fuse of a dormitory riot burned; Deke was ready with his blowtorch phrases.

"We oughta throw all these funny-talkin' greasers out!" and "when Mr. Henry goes off, it's going to be a long night for you reekans. Haw, haw!" He deferred to me because I had a reputation for not allowing any fighting on my shift.

Jonah disappointed Deke. His eyes blinking rapidly, he said gently, "Since we don't have any proof that Manuel took it, I'd rather not make any trouble over it. Just forget it." The tension in the room was let out like air from a pricked balloon. I loved him for it.

Now I recount this first acquaintance that I made with Jonah to show his initial attitude at the home so that it can be sharply contrasted with what took place some weeks later. On this second occasion the group had been scheduled to use the gymnasium for a few games of basketball. Owing to delays in lining up and getting ready, we were late arriving. The gym attendants, loath to stay overtime, turned us out. Most of the boys, including Deke, took it more or less good-naturedly; they'd get ready sooner next time. All except Jonah. He turned in anger to a smaller boy whom I'd had to call a number of times and screamed, "You little stupid motherfuckers are always messing up for the rest of us, just because you don't know how to play basketball!" As I turned around, his fist lashed out, decking the kid. I was both puzzled and embarrassed, because just that morning I had sent in a glowing account of Jonah's fine adjustment to group living. A radical change such as this is one of the ways that a boy will let you know that he needs more than routine care. The extent and degree of

Jonah's anger were far out of line from the provocation. Obviously there was something going on in him that needed seeing about.

Over the next couple of weeks we had several conversations from which I derived the following picture of his life prior to admission to the home. He was the oldest of three children. His mother had died when he was seven; his father had married again recently to a woman who Jonah felt was indifferent to him and his brothers. Jonah's antisocial acts soon began, and became serious enough for him to be remanded to our care. A contributing factor lay in the breakdown of his father. The man was drowning in booze and had actually been under psychiatric care for treatment of symptoms that had their origin in the bottle. Jonah plainly hated him. He described him in terms like "punk," "bum," "no good," "wine head," and so forth. The example that the poor man set for his boys was as dangerous to them as lacing their milk with arsenic.

In our dealings I tried to set a contrast with what he had been exposed to in his home. I listened to him, encouraged him, and was as comradely as the group situation would allow. As a measure of the long step we had taken together, he shortly announced that when he grew up, he wanted to go to college so that he could become a child counselor. After a conference with some of the other counselors, it was agreed that Jonah was qualified, in light of improved deportment and attitude, to be one of our "junior counselors," that is, an aid to the regular counselor. It was a job with some prestige and was eagerly sought after by the boys. I still retained some reservations about his ability to control his temper, but was willing to go along with the majority sentiment.

A fair question for any would-be counselor to ask at this point is how we knew that we were responsible for his improved relations with his peers. I have dealt somewhat with that topic earlier. Let it be enough to say now that when a boy chooses the vocation that you are following as the future one for himself, you can be assured that the model you are setting is at least doing him no harm. But there are better, subtler ways to tell.

Jonah was being given daily medication for an asthmatic condition. The schedule called for him to present himself at the infirmary each day at noon for his pills, and as far as I could tell, they seemed to lessen his susceptibility to attacks. Another problem that he was burdened with was bed-wetting, a rather frequent disorder of institutionalized boys. I had not made any big deal about it, but it was something of a nuisance to have to issue clean sheets and pajamas every morning. For some reason, the Night Service never seemed to get our night swimmers up on time. Some of the boys accused them of going to sleep themselves the moment they started their shift. Anyway, one day Jonah refused to take his medication. He was tired of swallowing pills, he said. Naturally, when he failed to show, the nurse, a very conscientious woman, called up and asked what gave with him. I did a little verbal arm twisting and got him to accompany me to the nurse's station to talk things over. On the way up Jonah confided that he was also diabetic and that he would gladly take pills for it, but he was tired of the asthma medicine. Now, as you may or may not know, diabetes in a child is a very serious matter—much more so than for an adult—and this being so, I wanted to know why he wasn't being treated for it. He replied that he had been sent over to the hospital for a glucose-tolerance test (a diabetes diagnostic test that requires a lot of blood samples to be drawn from the patient; it can be quite painful), but that no one had told him the results.

When we arrived at the infirmary, I asked the nurse about it, and she looked through his folder for a record of the test. It was negative. I was relieved. He was heartsick.

"Why in blazes do you want diabetes?" the nurse asked him when he insisted that he must be afflicted with it.

"Because that's the only reason I can think of that I wet the bed," he answered sullenly and with some embarrassment.

"You wet the bed?"

"Yes'm."

"There are a lot of reasons that a person may urinate in bed. Diabetes is just one of them. I'll make an appointment for you with the psychiatrist and he will help you get to the bottom of the problem."

"I'll be damned if I'm going to see any psychiatrist. I'm not crazy!" He glowered furiously at the nurse.

"That's the only thing I can suggest for you."

"Well, I'm not going to keep any appointment with any head doctor, so you might as well not set it up." The nurse looked at me, shrugging her shoulders.

"I'll tell you what, Mrs. ——. I'll take him on down to the dorm and talk to you later." When Jonah and I reached the staircase, I went into a long spiel about the fact that psychiatrists see hundreds of people for thousands of reasons besides their being "crazy," just as lots of people go to see chest doctors without having tuberculosis. "When a guy goes to see a psychiatrist for any reason, it puts him miles ahead of those who need to see one but can't screw up the guts to do so." As I talked, I watched him closely (always a good idea; never look out the window or study the wallpaper while you are trying to put a point across). His eyes were blinking in the same manner as the day he conciliated the loss of his cologne.

"I just don't want to be put in the same category as my father. He was always seeing psychiatrists, the crazy bastard."

"Believe me, Jonah, nobody is putting you into any class or category. Let's just say that for a thirteen-year-old boy to wet the bed is not exactly the expected thing, and maybe the psychiatrist can help you to find out why you're doing it. That's all the nurse had in mind. It has nothing to do with whether you're crazy, because obviously you're not." A few minutes more of my persuasion and he gave in. The appointment was made, he kept it, and I promptly forgot the whole matter until . . . until his adjustment to group living took a steady decline over the next few days, so much so that I began to get complaints from other counselors. There is no need to go into the different forms his breakdown took. It is enough to say that he began to act like a hood, with a special hostility for me. Gone was his interest in finishing school, gone was his enthusiasm for counseling (we had to demote him), gone was his amicability with his peers, and in its place was a surly, grudging reluctance to cooperate in any of the dormitory tasks. He was constantly grumbling: "This dorm is messed up; I'll be glad when I'm transferred." He finally was transferred to a larger center across town.

Now looking back at this case episode, what can we put our finger on as the cause of Jonah's going sour? As counselors we can think of a lot of reasons why a boy can suddenly become hostile, such as lack of news from home, loneliness, real or assumed slights from the counselors, uncertainty about his future, the cold atmosphere of any institution, fear, you name it. In Jonah's case, the big change in his attitude seemed to date from the episode with the nurse. It should have been clearer to me that he *needed* to believe in a physical cause for the bed-wetting rather than a psychological reason, which was what the nurse and I were trying to lay on him. The idea of a mental problem was poison; it put him in the same bag with his despised father. He felt debased by having to see the "shrinker." This is a common feeling among people who have an uninformed opinion of what psychiatry is all about. Convincing Jonah of the need for professional help was the province of the nurse or clinic physician, but since I had talked him into it, I should have been more aware of what it meant to him. It meant that he was weak like his father, and he couldn't forgive me for it.

So, lesson one: the Relations Method demands that the counselor keep in close touch with the feelings a boy expresses about something important to him, particularly his parents. Jonah and I got along well at the beginning because I was the opposite of what his father had been. We got along poorly at the end because of his nonacceptance of the idea of professional help (it linked him to Jonah senior) and my part in his decision to take it. This is not to say that he shouldn't have had help. But it was more within the responsibility of the nurse to lead him to it than it was in mine. The essence of relations counseling is to set an example, not to give advice. Not many of us are wise enough for that, anyway.

Well, then, you might ask, if we are not to give advice,

how are we to put over this "new set of values" you talk so much about? If we are really "salesmen," as you once referred to us, how can we sell this better life style without giving advice?

First of all, a salesman hustles a product that he is an expert on. Ford Motor Company would go out of business tomorrow morning if its franchise salesmen suddenly forgot all they knew about cars but were great authorities on the Hoover vacuum sweeper. I was not an expert on who needed to see a "shrink" or on how to cure bed-wetting. While it is true that the counselor must call to the attention of his supervisor or professional staff the rather big signs of disturbance within a boy, which I have outlined in a previous section, Jonah was showing none of them.

Well, then, what should have been done for Jonah, disregarding whether or not he saw a psychiatrist? First, the Night Service should have been geared into action, with express instructions to get him up at least twice during the night, say one o'clock and four. The evening crew should have been warned to be sure that he visited the restroom just before bedtime. The day counselor should have made follow-up checks (through his supervisor) to determine whether these duties were carried out. In my experience, several days of applying this kind of schedule on bed-wetters usually results in dry beds, for which everyone is grateful, most of all the child, and an occasional bonus. In not a few cases the boy will begin to get up himself at the scheduled times without being told. It is safer to have someone around to remind him, though. These are practical, nonpsychological moves that the group leader can make without waiting for professional aid.

As for the rest of it, values and behavior, you have to show in your personal style and attitude those traits that you want to create in them. This includes your whole self; neatness, hygiene, dress, temper, language, trust, dependability, the whole bit. For instance, it came as a shock to me that children's home residents put great stock in the punctuality of their counselors (just like the boss). They deeply resent (as some of them told me) the guy who drags in every morning twenty minutes late and expects them to double-time it out of bed to make up for his tardiness. And would you believe that some of them deduced quite correctly that a man who is always late is a man who really doesn't want to come at all? Let's face it, no car (not even my lemon) gets *that* many flat tires, and no public transit system (except New York's) breaks down *that* many times in a row. Would you also believe that some of them take your reluctance to show quite personally? I cannot stress too much that the kids are always sizing you up. Keep this in mind as you go from group relations to individual.

It occurred to me while doing a mental post-mortem on the above case that a conversation Jonah and I once had may have had more than incidental meaning. Shortly before his turn for the worse, he asked me what I was studying in college. I told him I was preparing for a career in clinical psychology. He then accused me of "using" psychology on them. I laughed. I didn't think he was serious.

"KEWPIE"

Of the instances of failure that I can recall in my management of boys, the one that gave me the greatest agony was the episode with Kewpie Owens. And yet, in itself, this case does not represent a fault of the Relations Method in theory or application, as did "Jonah," but is more typical of the bureaucratic elephant-walking that time and again the counselor will witness when he tries to apply reason, humanity, and his sense of commitment in the solution of human problems in some of the more backward institutions. This case study is a story of institutional inflexibility at its worst, a story that is being repeated over and over, not because the directors are inhuman or unintelligent, but because lack of imagination remains the dead weight that drags most such homes below what they could otherwise do for our refugees from the streets.

Kewpie Owens was a twelve-year-old, slender black youth who was sent to our children's home from a state mental hospital that refused to keep him any longer. (If it seems that I describe most of our kids as slender, it is not because of a lack of adjectives or vocabulary. That is the way they are. It is hard to find street children who are fat, or even healthy-looking.) He was plainly not "cured." But that is impossible, you might protest. No mental institution can turn a patient loose, particularly a child, if it is obvious that he needs further treatment. The answer is easy. He is simply *adjudged* cured and signed out to his parents; in Kewpie's case, his mother. She re-enrolled him in school, whence he was promptly suspended for incorrigibility and, of course, recommended for care in a mental facility. But since he had already, at age twelve, made the rounds of several state hospitals and was *known* to them, it was impossible to place him in one. He was an only child, and as his mother found it necessary to work and there was no one at home to care for him, she applied for his read-mission to a hospital, which dropped him into our lap.

Kewpie's outstanding symptom was uncontrollable, aggressive outbursts in which he would attack and try to inflict serious harm on those around him. In school, this involved his classmates, and on a number of occasions his teacher was threatened. When the bewildered principal asked him what the hell was going on, Kewpie's reply was that he felt dizzy just before the assault and then he wouldn't be able to control himself. He could, however, remember what he did in these attacks, so it wasn't a matter of sinking into a fugue or dream-like state. The problem was for those in the vicinity to be forewarned, and in this Kewpie was no help. He simply got dizzy and ... wham! The most serious thing he did while he was with us was to take a pair of shears and charge one of his dorm-mates. He missed the boy's jugular vein by a fraction of an inch.

Would you believe that when Kewpie was brought into the dorm, none of this background information was made available to us, his counselors? We were simply to take him and do the best we could with him on the assumption that he had no problems that were not common to most of the rest. In fact, when we were introduced, he offered a handshake and seemed rather anxious to cooperate.

His father had disappeared from home when Kewpie was about five, and his mother had borne no more children in the meantime. Ironically, the first notice that I took of something being awry with Kewpie was in his bed-wetting, although, as I have said, this problem is not all that uncommon among institutionalized boys. At first he tried to avoid detection by switching beds in the dark after he had bogged his bunk. Of course, the boys were not going to let him get away with that and quickly told us who the mysterious piddler on the hoof was.

On the positive side, Kewpie was the most cooperative youngster in the group when it came to making his bed and volunteering for cleaning chores, and I was on the verge of chalking up another big win for our Relations Method. In our initial talk, he had told me that the reason for his being here was that he was with some "bad boy" who had snatched some old lady's purse. The police had, quite mistakenly of course, picked him up. In the absence of his file, which I have already outlined, I had to take his word for it, and besides, with the exception of his bed-wetting, his conduct was exemplary.

Then day four arrived. To our misfortune, one of the boys had pilfered the office desk and removed a box of paperclips and a handful of rubber bands. A rubber slingshot and a pocketful of paperclips was to Kewpie what bullets and a Tommy gun were to Machine Gun Kelly. Long after the fun had gone out of the paperclip battles and the other boys had given them up, Kewpie kept blasting them in the face and backside. It did no good to talk about possible dangers to their eyesight. He was having too much fun to quit.

The incident of the slingshot seemed to be a catalyst for the emergence of Kewpie's aggressive nature. The next day a rather effeminate white youngster moment-arily blocked his view of the television. Without a word he rose and slammed a hard punch into the boy's stomach. When I admonished Kewpie about it, he copped the race plea; the boy had called him some kind of racial "name." Again he seemed not to give a damn about anyone else's well-being. Even though we still had not been told anything about his past history, I decided that it was about time our resident psychologist had a look at him. We also prevailed upon his social worker to give us whatever background data she had. It was only then, through her efforts, that we learned of his sojourns in the state hospitals. Now I knew why my one-on-one relations interviews were having so little effect.

Meanwhile his attacks on other boys, particularly white boys, increased. This doesn't mean that he ignored the blacks. But since white kids were a definite minority in the dorm, Kewpie had the presence of mind to concentrate on them. There was always a larger black boy to rescue him should the going get rough.

We strongly considered requesting that Kewpie be transferred to another group, but declined out of sympathy for whoever the receiving counselor might be. We immediately prevailed upon the social worker to gear up the bureaucratic machinery to have Kewpie treated on a short-term, acute-illness basis at the city's largest receiving hospital. She answered that it might take several weeks to have that done. The psychiatrist who had interviewed him and heard of the increasing havoc in the dorm prescribed daily dosages of Mellaril, a tranquilizer. It would be given at four-hour intervals until bedtime, when he would get a double quantity to carry though the night. Of course, this would not help the bed-wetting; the slight chance there was of Kewpie waking up to go to the bathroom before flooding his flop would go right down the drain.

Before the doctor's orders could be put into effect, Kewpie's antics took an ominous turn. In addition to the constant hazing of the other boys, he now began to take on counselors, first with a tossed shoe or book, later with threats to throw chairs. All that was needed to set him off was for one of us to censure him about abusing the other boys.

I might state parenthetically that Kewpie was one of the types mentioned earlier whom the group-relations method of control will not faze. It never works with children in acute psychosis (actively mentally disturbed) or who are psychopathic (governed strictly by pleasure principle). Kewpie was, according to the psychiatrist, psychotic. In addition to the medication, the psychiatrist recommended that he be moved to a more stable dormitory. He had no way of knowing that ours *was* a more stable dorm than most of the others.

According to the home's rules, we were supposed to keep daily records of whatever went on in the dorm and to submit special reports of anything outstanding. Naturally Kewpie's behavior began to fill page after page of the log book and to be the subject of numberless special reports, particularly after he started to strike out at counselors. The administration couldn't be sparked into action. The word on getting him into a mental facility was *nothing doing*. They were jammed. We would have to do what we could on the premises, maybe increase his dosage of the happy pills. A word about those pills. After he had gulped them down, a funny thing happened on his way to tranquillity. Instead of calming him down, the tranquilizer jacked him up! If he had been only moderately obnoxious before taking them, he became the devil incarnate afterward. When, to our dismay, we found this out, we did two things. We requested through the clinic nurse that the kind of medication be changed . . . and found out how little faith is put in the observations of ordinary laymen. After all, if the pharmacopoeia says that drug X is supposed to mellow an overactive patient, then, by God, that patient has been mellowed, even if he *is* swinging from the chandelier, throwing lightbulbs down at you. So Mellaril it was going to stay. By now I was starting to feel the first twinges of panic and momentarily considered asking Kewpie to pass *me* his pills, since they weren't doing *him* any good. Then my partner suggested telling him the effect that his pills were *supposed* to have and that to keep from possibly getting drowsy and falling over the furniture and hurting himself, he should lie down and sleep until the effects(!) wore off. It seemed to work. In some instances a good con job will beat the socks off chemistry.

Meanwhile, back in the supervisor's office our special

reports were piling up . . . in our mailboxes. Whoever was supposed to read them either hadn't or had and wasn't impressed by them, and so our bright little suggestions for putting Kewpie somewhere else in the home with a nice big counselor all his own that he could play with, or finding some mental facility somewhere that hadn't heard of him yet, or for changing his medicine, or for getting him short-term treatment in a hospital were bounced right back at us, unheeded and unacknowledged.

Then Kewpie made a mistake. He jumped a supervisor and followed it up by trying to assault the assistant director (he had already taken a swing at his social worker, but they, like counselors, don't count). What happened next was equivalent to an elephant stampede. Watching a flatulent bureaucratic machine roar into action after one of its high priests is attacked is like seeing the launching of Apollo 15, the christening of the S.S. *United States,* Native Dancer rounding the last turn, Jimmy Brown carrying eight tacklers into the end zone, and Ford getting a "better idea"—all in a flash. I'll never forget that last wild scene in the supervisor's office: Kewpie backed up into a corner blazing away at the supervisor and me with ashtrays and paperweights; the supervisor, a brave and sizeable woman, threatening to cream him, and me hiding behind her. Thank God his aim was lousy. He could have hurt her.

In ten minutes flat a psychiatrist was hustled over from the next-door hospital; commitment papers were already filled out for him to sign when he arrived, and within an hour a city vehicle arrived to deliver Kewpie to a psychiatric ward. In ten minutes of frenzy he had accomplished what we, in two weeks of report writing, had failed to do—wake up the energies of the home and get something done for him.

Coincidentally I learned, should the necessity ever again arise, the best way to get a violent patient admitted to a city mental hospital. Don't, repeat, don't try to calm him down. Throw his Mellaril right out the window. In fact, tell him he's a sissy if he doesn't keep acting up. Why? Suppose you do get him pacified before you take him to the happy house. When the desk clerk looks up and sees this perfectly calm (drugged) person that you've got a half nelson on, her first question is, "What's wrong with him?" Or, "Why are you holding him like that?" "He's uncontrollable," you answer; "Went berserk about an hour ago and tried to take my head off with his little hatchet—after he had torn up the dormitory and battered two counselors into your emergency room." "But he looks all right now," comes the answer. "Sorry, but we can't admit him unless he is actively showing the symptoms you are talking about. Bring him back when he's giving you trouble."

Then she goes back to filing her nails. So you take your sleeping volcano back to the padded station wagon and wait for the next eruption, praying that it comes on your day off. So we didn't tranquilize Kewpie, not that it would have done any good. When the committing psychiatrist came in, we were doing our Godzilla versus King Kong act on the floor. Sorry about that, old buddy. My only other regret is that you couldn't get to the guy who "ran" the place.

"DEE"

In all my years of counseling, Dee Williams was the only boy I ever met who managed to make all of his peers and most of the staff despise him. A slender, light-complexioned, handsome youth of sixteen, he swaggered into the dorm one day on a neglect petition. According to his office file, he had been living with his grandmother for the past three years, but when the old lady became ill and had to be hospitalized, Dee left the small apartment they had been sharing and started to live in the streets with some of his friends, older teenagers, and men who had been surviving by their wits in the barbarizing Harlem jungle for most of their lives.

For them school was, of course, a laugh. The skills they developed were the hard-won, practical ones acquired in subway terminals where tired old ladies hauled their creaking frames up the stairs, practically begging to be sapped and robbed. They sharpened those skills in darkened·doorways when drunks, lurching along after a hard night's drinking, offered themselves up to the merciless attentions of Dee and his companions. They added color and excitement to them in the basements of abandoned buildings, where the hallucinizing, care-chasing "fixes" coursed from needles into distended veins and wafted from vaporizers into expectant nostrils. And the final flourish was added to the skills on the rooftops of Harlem's tenements, where teenage and sub-teen girls were dragged to be initiated into the ritual of gang rape (called "running a train up Thigh Alley"). At age sixteen Dee had seen and done a lifetime course in the dysculture of street living, and he had graduated with honors. His eyes, brown and intelligent, were the eyes of an old, old man.

Miraculously he hadn't been caught. The formal charge was vagrancy, which, because he was a minor, was changed to neglect. No one seemed to be responsible for him. The old lady was wheezing her lungs away in Harlem Hospital.

As was my custom with any new admission, I called Dee aside to talk with him on that first day. My first impression was the ease with which he slid into the game that boys think nosy counselors want to play when we ask about their plans for the future. He wanted to "make something" of himself. A boy playing this game will usually describe something fairly grandiose, with a title that fairly crackles with crisp, starched collars and a pocketful of pens. I make this point to put you on your toes. Don't rock back on your heels when you hear something in this vein. In fact, you should always encourage him in these projects unless it is something destructive, like blowing up public monuments. Because it could be that he really is sincere; give him the benefit of any doubt. Future planning is the best new trait that he could develop. So, though it was obvious that Dee thought he was snowing me, I went along with it.

The group into which he was enrolled had been worked into a stable dorm society. The boys held regular meetings and friction was minimal. There were twelve of them, white, Puerto Rican, and black. Would you believe, in these hateful times, that there was real brotherhood among them? For example, one boy, a white youngster who was retarded (someone had to tie his shoes for him—after they had shown him which foot to put each one on), was glacially slow in getting ready for the day's routines. One of the black kids, a boy from Alabama who was as mischievous as an imp but likable as hell, always volunteered to make his bed for him and help him find his clothes. To be honest, I don't think I ever quite got over my astonishment that this was a Southern black child and a white boy in (now) unlikely fraternity. I thought of how much smarter both of them were than we old folks. But that is the kind of group it was.

Dee's entrance into their ranks was tantamount to a thunderbolt hitting a herd of grazing buffalo. He stampeded them . . . toward himself. The friction began the morning of his second day. He started things off with a loud, profane complaint to me that some of his belongings had been taken by one of these "snotty-nosed punks," and if he ever laid hands on him he was going to "kick some ass." As there were women counselors present, I asked Dee to tone down the language. He wanted to know what the hell for. What made the difference if some of those "so-called ladies" heard it? They could kiss his ass.

"Well, in the first place," I began, my anger aroused, "I doubt very seriously whether you would want anyone to talk like this in front of your mother."

"You kidding? I'd tell my mother to do the same thing if she was here."

"What?"

"You heard me. If my mother was here right now, I'd tell her to kiss my ass. I don't care any more about her than I would about a stranger!"

Now when a black youngster expresses disdain or even hatred for his father, it isn't news. Many of them haven't seen the guy for a while. And in normal circumstances the mother becomes the chief repository of his loyalty. Dee's circumstances were anything but normal, even by the skewed standards of our detention center. So these shafts aimed at his mother rocked me.

"How can you say something like that?"

"Easy. My mother never did anything for me."

"What do you mean?"

"I mean she left me when I was a baby. My grandmother raised me," he answered evenly.

"Was she sick or something?"

"No. She just didn't want me. The lousy bitch didn't even know who my father was. My grandmother said she didn't even want to bring me home from the hospital. Grandma had to come get me."

"I see." I got the picture, all right. A young girl in trouble with her family and the world, knocked up by some character—she didn't know who—and left to sink or swim as she was able. She had decided to stroke without a baby to weight her down.

Before noon of that day, Dee had cornered one of the boys in the restroom and pummeled him, claiming that he had found his belt among the boy's goods in his locker. The kid he had licked happened to be one of the more popular boys, and there were angry mutterings in the group about ganging up on Dee. I took him aside and blasted him about taking things into his own hands. Going into other people's lockers and meting out punishment, if there was to be any, was my job, I told him.

"Well, you'd better do your job, because I'm not going to take anything off these guys."

Such was the flavor of the dorm's first taste of Dee. And the taste didn't improve with later samplings. Our next set-to came when he threatened the unit director, who happened to be a woman. This was brought on by her refusal to give him permission to leave the building before the normal three-day probationary period was up. The director, a doughty little person who was graced with the patience of Job, listened for ten minutes to a harangue from Dee in which he told her what an all-purpose slob she was and how lucky she was that he didn't feel like knocking her on her can for not letting him out. Her only reply, as I recall it, was that she didn't believe that Dee hated her so much. He assured her that he did.

Faced by a tornado like Dee, who insisted on stirring up the potential for violence which is always present in a boys' group, my first hope was to dampen the exchanges that flew back and forth between him and the other kids. The best way to do this was to remove the ostensible cause of the friction, his fear that they were out to steal something from him. I showed him the closet where we kept the children's valuables and assured him that, to date, no one had managed to pick the lock. This done, I began to talk to him about the similarities between himself and the others, mentioning the fact that most of them were without intact families on the outside and that all suffered from rather common problems. I tried, in other words, to forge a link between him and his peers, and in a few days the tension eased. Dee and his new "family" were at least on speaking, rather than shouting, terms. A few days later—could I believe my eyes?—I saw him help one of the smaller fry fold up his cot. The days of whine and poses seemed to be over. So far so good.

I can't take the credit for that first truce. As I stated in the beginning, the dorm was a stable one when Dee arrived. It would have been impossible to work with him if the group were a riotous one. The point is that it is much easier to integrate a youngster into a smoothly functioning society than into one that is still in the anarchy stage. So most of the quieting influence on Dee came from the group tone itself.

Up to now, Dee was apparently reconciled to group life but not to adult authority. One day I came to work and was told that one of my co-workers had had to wrestle him down in a flare-up over—you guessed it—disputed ownership of a notebook. I didn't get too much excited, because in any process of personal change a boy is likely to take a step backward occasionally. I continued my individual sessions with him, which were nothing more than little five- or ten-minute chats in which we talked about him and his future. He had stopped trying to snow me. I now felt confident enough to suggest that the day might come, after he was an adult and successful, when he might possibly be able to forgive his mother. He didn't answer one way or the other, but I was encouraged that he didn't curse her this time. We had come a long way.

Our last big step forward came about as the result of his school attendance, or lack of it. For several weeks Dee had been enrolled at a high school several blocks away. We sent him out every morning with his subway fare and assumed, rather naively, that he was getting there. The school truant officer informed us that our little angel had shown exactly three times in three weeks. The story he gave me when I asked him about it was that he had been threatened by some of the boys there, and to keep out of trouble he had simply not gone back after the first week. Given the condition of some of Manhattan's public schools, Dee's story about the bullies was a plausible one. I asked why he hadn't complained to the principal or some other school official, or told one of us about it. His answer was that he would rather be responsible for himself and not depend on someone else to look out for him. At my urging, he promised to go back to school and stay this time. Of course, within a few weeks the truancy cycle started again. Now while I believed the part of his story about the boys being out to get him, I didn't accept it as the principal cause of his staying away. He was too street-wise, too hip to be intimidated by youngsters in public schools who were straight enough to attend regularly. Furthermore, we had other kids in the same school who were not bothered at all. So this time I gave him a far different reception from the first one. To put it bluntly, I raised hell.

Now what is the point of my taking you through this wordy recounting leading up to Dee's and my great "step forward"? Just this. Until now, Dee had never accepted a chewing-out from any adult, parents (such as they were) included, let alone some guy in a children's home. He had been a one-hundred-and-thirty-pound bundle of hostility. Add to this the fact that I had never before so much as raised my voice to him. But today I was ticked off and let him have it. Loudly. I ranted like some backwoods preacher calling the sinners to repent. Incidentally, I consider the ability to give a hell-fire and brimstone lecture to wayward youngsters a vital part of the counselor's bag. The important thing is to know when to use it. There are no preachers in my family, but I'm a thing of beauty when I get wound up. Well, anyway, would you believe that Dee, the kid with the two-by-four chip on his shoulder, endured the entire riot act in meek silence, his head hung low, answering "Yes, sir," and "No, sir," the few times I paused for air?

Of course, the answer to this attitude is fairly obvious. In his outside experiences, Dee had skipped boyhood. In his relationship with me he had discovered how wide the gap was between manhood and what he had previously (mis)taken to be manhood. But even more essential is the fact that he believed that I was acting in his behalf, as indeed I was. He took the upbraiding from me because he and I knew that I was his ally in this war against his self-destructive habits. He was now ready to be led.

The point at which a youngster is "ready" varies from one boy to the next, and with the Relations Method you can pick up those times. For Jonah it was at the beginning rather than later in our talks. Children also vary in the extent of forceful guidance that they will accept. Most of them can relate to extremely aggressive counseling (such as Dee was now hearing), provided it is being done for them and not to them. Good relations between counselor and boy break down when this trust is violated or when the counselor somehow fails to communicate to the youngster his sincere desire to help him improve and to live a better life.

What happened next between us? Nothing. Since in our home, as in most others, the needs of the administration and scheduling are served rather than the boys', I was transferred to another group, so his personal confidant was gone. The streets did the rest.

Now let me kill two birds with one stone. Let me recount the things that we should have done for Dee, while stipulating that these were the things we did not do. We should have had someone *accompany him* to the school to see exactly what the difficulty was and to work out some arrangement with school officials that would have relieved the problem of bullies and threats, if there actually was one. Then there should have been a *follow-up* to check on our proposed solutions so that we could alter them if need be. At the same time there should have been *daily checks* with both the truant officer and Dee to ascertain the regularity of his attendance. Having now induced Dee to discard some of his old coping stratagems, someone should have moved in with *new suggestions* for "making it," since he was now obviously ready to listen. And finally, perhaps most important, we should have found a part-time job for him as an important new direction in his development. We did none of these things. The level of hatred for him among some of the staff who were still reacting to his early obnoxiousness thwarted an outlook like this. The next time I heard about him, my supervisor told me that he had been arrested near his school for possession of narcotics, although it was not known whether he was actually selling them or was a user. This was the sorry postscript to a story that could have ended differently.

"VIO" THE MAGNIFICENT

Vio Martinez was a ten-year-old Puerto Rican boy who had been brought into the children's shelter by the police as a runaway. They had picked him up in a Latin section of Brooklyn and contacted his stepmother, who had put out the call on him. But it was days before she came to the children's home to see him, and when she did, she didn't take him back. Vio had been in the dorm for about a month when I first saw him.

He was rather short for his age but wiry and muscular. He had the dark-eyed good looks that Latin children are blessed with. He also had the savage temper that many urban kids are cursed with. Because of his age, he was placed in the junior section of our Intake dormitory. That is where we collided. I was substituting for the regular counselor, who was on vacation. He knew when to leave. In all I had five fights involving Vio. Two were with him; three were for him.

There were fourteen boys in this group and they got along with the normal number of arguments, friendships, fights, and making-ups that you come to expect in groups of this pre-teen age range. The daily routine was simple and unchanging. Arise at seven, make up the beds, collect towels and toothbrushes, and line up for showers. Afterward, breakfast and school. On Saturdays there was a downtown trip to a movie, and on Sundays church and an afternoon show in our auditorium.

It wasn't long on that first day before I took note of Vio. In fact, we lasted exactly thirty minutes before the falling out. The reason was a fight. Someone had the nerve to shove him in line or something. I have seen hundreds of fights between sub-teen boys and they usually end fairly quickly, after a couple of good shots are landed. But not with this new boy. I had never seen such cold determination in a child's face; he seemed to want to kill the other boy. He fought as if he were possessed, pursued by an urgency that said, Kill or die. When I shoved through the crowd of boys around them, Vio had pinned the hapless other kid to the floor and was slamming pile-driver punches into his face. When I pulled him off, he pulled the boy up with him with one hand and kept flailing him with the other. His strength was, to say the least, surprising. His victim was a wreck, and I had to take him up to the infirmary. On the way, I dropped a furious, screaming Vio off at the director's office.

When I got back down, I discovered that he had something else besides fast fists; it was a great imagination. According to what he told the director, I had jumped him simply because he was defending himself. I'd better keep my hands off him or his father would take care of me.

"Where is your father?" Miss J——, the director, asked. Vio's face underwent a quick transformation from a scowl to a kind of sad, questioning look.

"I—I don't know," he answered. "But he's coming to get me and take me to live with him."

"When will that be?" I asked hopefully.

"I don't want to talk to you!" he flared. Miss J—— sent him back to the dorm and said to me, "Don't worry about it. We have had plenty of experience with him. He was here last year."

"What for, dynamiting the Bank of America?"

"No," she laughed. "He ran away and his stepmother called the police. They picked him up, same as this time. He told us so many stories, really wild stories, about her that we sent a social worker out to look into the family situation. A lot of it he had made up—that's how we know he's a liar—but some of what he told us about the home thing is true." I asked to see the report.

His mother had died when he was six, and for a time he lived with his father, a former professional boxer. In the first couple of years following his mother's death, Vio and his father got along well. They lived in a comfortable apartment in Brooklyn, and were occasionally visited by the boy's grandparents.

Trouble first began when Vio's father married again, this time to a woman with two children of her own. Vio was nine and a half. His record showed that at about that time he ran away from home and was brought into a city children's facility. After several weeks he was released to his father and returned to the now expanded family. He stayed with them more or less unhappily until, after being chastised by his father on the word of his stepmother, he ran away once again and was brought back to our shelter.

The next fight that Vio and I had came the next morning at the breakfast table. According to the rules, the boys were to remain seated and not converse with anyone at the next table, though it was all right to talk at the table where you were sitting. Naturally, Vio just had to tell a boy at the next table something of burning importance, so he turned around to chat with him. Not wanting a repetition of yesterday's friction, I tried to ignore it, but when it seemed like they were going to turn it into a two-way filibuster, I asked them to turn around and eat. The other boy complied, but Vio said, "Fuck you" ... and the rumble was on. Down the stairs we went, me holding and shaking him, him calling down God's maledictions on me, my family, my ancestors, and any connected with us by blood or appearance.

I had, of course, heard people curse before, usually men in stag situations like ball games, prelims to fist fights, poker games, and in good-natured joshing. But compared with the string of foulness let loose by Vio, that language was as pure as the Boy Scout pledge. I was both startled and impressed, because it was the first time I'd heard anyone, child or adult, swear for three minutes without repeating a curse word. This takes some doing. One memorable warning that he gave me was that when his father finished with me, I'd be s——g pickles. The imagery of that one gave me a little pain just thinking about it.

Nonetheless, for the second straight day I hauled him down to the director's office for another cooling-off period. After about thirty minutes he returned to the dorm, his tears dried into dirty streaks down his cheeks. As the rest of the boys had by now gone up to school, he and I were left to ourselves. I wrote in the log book but kept an eye on him all the time. He disconsolately plopped down in front of the TV. Though I was writing the day's agenda, the wheels in my head were in another groove. The question was, of course, how to get across that barbed-wire barrier that Vio had thrown up. With him there was no "common ground" that I could get on with him, a step that is essential in relations. Even though I knew his past history from the office file, it wouldn't do much good, I thought, to bring any of it up. Most of it was painful for him, anyway. But there had to be something, some bit of like experience that he, an angry young Puerto Rican, and I, an older, perplexed black man, could hook onto as human beings. Then I thought of his vocabulary of profanity. I called him over to the desk.

"What do you want?" he asked, his hands jammed into his denim pockets, a frown knotting his brow. When I spoke, I kept my eyes down on the log book, pretending to be only mildly distracted from what I was writing. It is a good psychological ploy because it makes the person you're talking with think that you're almost too busy to be bothered with him. It motivates him to respond by talking. No one likes to be upstaged by a note pad. I use it when a boy is angry with me. If he refuses to talk, you just go on writing, glancing up now and then as though you're surprised that he's still there.

"I was just thinking, where did you learn all those curse words?" I asked, putting a note of admiration into my voice. "I mean, they were really something."

"I learned them here," he answered. I kept jotting with the pen. After a long pause, I said, "What?"

"I learned them here. The first time I came I didn't know how to curse. My father wouldn't let me talk like that," he said, his frown easing a bit.

"Well, who taught you all those words? I haven't heard anyone talk like that."

"The counselors. I used to listen to them when they talked to each other, and sometimes when they talked to us they would curse. So I just remembered."

"Say, that's pretty good! I mean your being able to remember so much. Are you that good at remembering in school?" My pen was working again.

"Sure, when I go. But I don't go to school any more."

"Oh, why not?"

"They don't like me up there. I got suspended." I laid the pen down.

"Why?"

" 'Cause I kept getting into fights and bawling out the teacher, so I got suspended."

"Hummm. Tell me, when you bawled out the teacher, did you talk the way you talked to me this morning?" I looked hard at him, which is to say, tried to engage his eyes. You have to go through this a few times before it is driven home to you how important eye contact is in getting a straight story from a child. For the first time since I'd known him, Vio smiled and looked away in embarrassment. "You did talk like that, right?"

"Yes."

I knew I had him. I went back to my writing. When the fish is nibbling, you don't yank the line. I glanced up at his baggy trousers, the soiled polo shirt.

"Why don't you put on some other clothes? The ones you have on now are pretty far gone."

"These are all I've got. Besides, I like them." I stopped writing again and looked up wide-eyed, as though the idea had just occurred to me. "Say, I'll bet you that I could find you a suit of clothes that would make you look

as good as the guys who went out to school this morning.
Yeah, I bet you'd look all right in a tie, a sport coat, and
some sharp creased slacks." I jumped up before he could
protest and went rummaging through the closet. It took
some doing, but I came up with an outfit his size. When
you're working with a kid who may be a little reluctant to
let you operate, you don't ask him, "Would you like to put
this on?" or something dumb like that. You go right
ahead as though you and he have already agreed upon it.
So I rushed over with the shirt and held it up against him.

"Hey, that's mellow!" I said. "Come over to the mirror
and see how great it's going to look." He came, looked,
and grinned. The rest was easy.

"You know something, Vio," I said, as he stood looking
at himself in the mirror and fingering his tie.

"What?"

"I found you the clothes, right? When you thought
there weren't any around for you, right?" Not exactly true,
but I'm no Boy Scout.

"Right."

"Okay. Now you said you don't like school, right? I'll
bet you that if you go to school and *listen* and do your
work, you *will* like it."

"No! No, I won't."

"Now wait. I was right about the clothes, wasn't I?" He
looked at himself again, and there was no denying that
he was as sharp as a tack in them.

"Yes."

"Well, then, you *know* I'm right about school. Tell you
what," I said, stooping so that our eye levels were equal,
"I'll take you up to class this morning and you just give it
a try. In other words, don't bother any of your classmates
or curse out the teacher. And if, after a couple of days,
you still don't like it, I won't say anything more about
it." Here, I was gambling; and also lying a little. If he
had come back after two days saying that he still didn't
like it, I'd have made a different bargain to get him to
stay in school—where a ten-year-old belongs.

"But they *don't want* me!"

"Yes, they do want you. The trouble is, they don't
understand all those swear words the way you and I do.

They also may not understand your fighting. Tell you what, you and I will work on your cursing and fighting down here in the dorm, so maybe you won't do it in the classroom. But for this morning, just *try* to last. Okay?" He looked at me, searching my face. "Deal?" I said, sticking out my hand. "Deal." We shook.

To be frank, I knew nothing about the institution's school, whether the teachers were lively and sympathetic with the boys or whether they were just warmed-over bodies sent by the board to call the roll. I also didn't know the exact nature of Vio's offense in class and the official reason for his suspension. But whatever the truth was, I was convinced that he needed and deserved to be in class.

The three battles I had to get Vio back in school began in the principal's office. We went there first because I thought it wise to find out from "the horse's mouth" why he'd been kicked out. The horse almost kicked both of us out of the office. "What's he doing here?" Mrs. G——, the principal, asked the moment she saw him. I asked him to wait outside while I talked with her. He looked doubtful but obeyed. I told her that I wanted to know what had happened in Vio's previous enrollment that was so bad he had to be deprived of an education. It turned out to be about the way he had described it. He had deprived himself, she said, by trying to take over Mrs. Jones' class. When I told her that he and I had talked it over and that he deserved another chance, she said it was up to the teacher he was last enrolled with. "Let me take you down to her class."

When the three of us arrived at the classroom, the principal stuck her head in the door and said, "We're re-enrolling Vio. It's understood that you are to take no nonsense." With these kind words, she left us.

If ever I have seen hate settle onto a person's face, like a carrion bird weighting down a tree limb, it settled on the face of Vio's former teacher when she looked at him. She was a slender, attractive black woman, and her facial expression became even darker when she turned from the chalk board to look at us.

"He can't come in here, " she said. I felt like someone

had dropped an icicle down my back; that's how cold the look was.

"See, I told you," Vio said, edging toward the door.

"Wait, let me talk to her," I told him. I walked to the front of the room and spoke in a tone low enough so that the class couldn't make out what I was saying. I told her that I had been with Vio for only two days and that I knew from hard experience how mad he could make a person. "But he and I have made this deal—"

"He isn't supposed to be in here, anyway," she said, cutting me off. "His group has moved over across the hall to Miss Carter. They're on a new segment of the course."

"Oh, is that so?" I didn't believe her. Her hatred for him was too evident, and besides, the principal had brought us to her, not across the hall.

"Even if I wanted to take him, I couldn't," she insisted, "because he doesn't belong here."

"I see. Then I'll take him across the hall. I'm sure that I can get him in *somewhere*." I explained to Vio that his group had moved and that was the only reason he couldn't go back to Mrs. Jones' class.

The third battle was with Miss Carter, a young white teacher who had apparently heard about Vio from Mrs. Jones or the principal. The stories must have been pretty vivid, because as soon as I gave her his name, she froze. Vio, a veteran by now, read her grimace accurately and headed for the door.

"Wait," I said. "You promised me that you'd try. I'm going to keep my promise to you." I turned back to the teacher and went through my spiel again.

"Okay, I'll take him, but one false move and—"

"You don't need to worry about that. He and I have a bargain going." Before I left, I took Vio's hand and shook it, saying, "Just this once, try! Okay?"

"Okay," he answered. I felt like I had left him to wolves.

The rest of the morning I fretted and muttered to myself and paced the dormitory floor, expecting the teacher or principal or director to burst in with a demand that I come and get Vio, who must surely be tearing up the classroom by now. It never happened. At twelve, lunchtime, I stood out in the hallway waiting for the boys to come in from their classes. Then I saw Miss Carter. She had Vio in tow. I began to think of explanations to give her for his new misbehavior until I saw that she had her arm around his shoulder.

"I just had to come down and tell you," she said brightly, "how wonderful Vio was this morning!"

His grin was the size of a billboard. I exhaled and realized that I hadn't breathed since I first saw them coming.

"Really," she went on, "he was the smartest thing in the room. He was magnificent!"

"What did I tell you?" I said. "And what did I tell *you*, Vio? Pretty good, right?"

"Right."

From then on, school was no problem for him. I continued to talk with his teacher and she marveled at his prodigious memory. And not only could he remember, he understood. He also understood what I was trying to do with him. One day I mentioned that he was doing great in school and in the dining hall. He agreed. (Modesty was not one of Vio's traits.) I then asked what he supposed the next thing was we would work on. Without looking up from the picture he was drawing, he answered, "My behavior here in the dorm. I have to stop hitting people, right?"

"Right," I answered. And we started.

Vio never became an angel. No boy should be. But the bitter, hostile, unforgiving exterior that I first met melted away in the course of our talks together. When I was transferred shortly afterward, there was still the question of lying, but now it *was* a question rather than accepted fact. He still needed delicate handling, in my opinion, in the same way that an open wound or a broken bone needs gentle treatment. He didn't get it. The one other counselor who enjoyed a good man-boy relationship with Vio became ill and had to stay out an additional two weeks, and when he returned Vio had been moved to another dorm, where he had to start all over again.

Fortunately, he was soon discharged to the custody of his grandmother, who took him back to San Juan. I don't know what became of him, but I'm not hopeful. In San Juan there is poverty that matches Harlem's or Brownsville's. What is likely to happen to an already bruised boy thrown into either of these two cauldrons will probably befall Vio also. I would like to think otherwise, but the world seems to have run out of miracles.

EPILOGUE

It isn't necessary for me to review the stages Vio and I went through in our development of trust. The stage for this development was set the first time I held that shirt up against him for size. It was the first time that I ever used the subject of curse words as a beginning point in relations. The important thing was that he was able to use the time and educational opportunities there far better than he would have if he'd stayed choked with bitterness. A trouble with this process in many instances is the shortness of the time the boy and the counselor have. On a number of occasions it has happened that a boy who was being brought out of his coccoon of mistrust by a counselor was discharged or moved out of that counselor's influence to another dorm. When this happens, the process may (but not necessarily) be stopped. If the new counselors are of the old, non-relations, rock 'em, sock 'em type, there may be a return to the old brutal attitude of the survival of the fittest.

In the ideal situation, the new boy is enrolled in a dormitory with a company of other boys (his new "family") and a staff of counselors, and remains there for the term of his residency (or sentence). Of course, the length of the boy's stay depends on the kind of juvenile institution it is and on the nature of the reason he is there. Whatever the type of center, if the new admission enters an already stable dormitory, his adjustment to the group is much easier than if there is a high turnover rate. The latter condition results if someone in administration gets the bright idea that all new admissions should be put together in one dorm, as happened in a New York center where I once worked. What you get (and what we got) is sustained anarchy. Owing to the constant influx of new members and removal of old ones, the counselors almost never had control. It was a constant battle of wit and muscle, with uncertain outcome. Listen to the report of one counselor who had to spend a weekend in November, 1969, with them and recorded her(!) experience in the log book:

"Help! I am sick of being assigned to Intake by myself with not enough help to maintain order. I arrived at 7:00 A.M. and it looked like a tornado had hit the place. There were shoes everywhere, an overturned locker and clothes laying all around.

"When I asked the boys to get up for showers and breakfast, half of them stayed in bed, so I took the ones who got up with me. When we got back from showers, a shoe battle had broken out between two bunches of them and since I was alone as there was no supervisor around, there was nothing I could do. Then the boys who went for showers complained that their clothes had been stolen.

"As a result of all this turmoil, we were late for breakfast and caught the devil from the kitchen.

"The names of the boys who caused most of the ruckus are . . ." and on the lament goes. This report is typical of those written by the worn-out counselors who had to serve in that idiotic scheme. Listen to another, somehow amusing log note written by a young white counselor who had been left to the weekend mercies of Intake and who walked off the job. It was a Saturday night in January, 1970, in the same dorm as the above.

"I've had it! I know when I am able to function in a job and when I'm not. Tonight when my co-worker and I told the boys in Intake-3 to get ready for bed, they turned out the lights and started throwing shoes at us. This bunch of boys is absolutely without any discipline whatsoever. I have never seen kids act this wild.

"So I am leaving as of 9:00 p.m. They are still having shoe fights in there. I am through trying to tackle things that I can't handle!" To his partner's credit, a white, hippie-type girl, she stayed till the bitter end.

An even worse practice than putting all new boys into one unit is placing several members of the same street gang into a dormitory. This happened in an Ohio center in the spring of 1968 (and probably several times before and since), to which a crew from Cleveland's Hough

Avenue was sent for street brawling and assault. When they arrived at our shelter, a place supposedly for diagnosis of psychological problems, they were all quartered in the same dormitory. I don't need to tell you the kinds of problems those counselors and the other boys soon began to have.

So the march of the elephants goes on. I propose an alternate path, one that may get us out of the quicksand that we are now bogged down in. The boys who enter our youth institutions are beset by two kinds of social problems. One is their street (and family) background. I have spoken of the contribution that our country's racist (for black) and government (for black and white) economic policies make to that problem. Unfortunately, I do not know how to reverse these policies; America seems determined to keep her date with disaster.

The other problem is that which is generated within the youth houses by faulty administrative policies. We can reverse these. I have used scores of pages showing how we may reverse them.

The most important employees in these institutions are the men who face the boys day by day, hour by hour. These are the lowest-paid employees in the system. Also, they are less well trained to carry out their duties than the mail clerk or office steno. And in terms of the administrative hierarchy, they have less authority than anyone in the system. The cost in morale of the counselors is shown by the quality of the men who stay in this line of work. These facts are not lost on the boys. One of them used to tease me when I advised him to go to school, saying, "I don't need an education, Mr. Henry. I want to be a counselor."

So, to answer some friends who asked me how I would change things within the present budgetary limitations—since no new money is being allocated on any government level for rehabilitative work—my answer is, We'll have to work with what we've got. The first thing I would do in a home that has the problems I outlined in the preceding chapters is to require each counselor to attend and pass four of the job courses. One would be Child Development from infancy through early adulthood and another, taught at the same time, would be Modern Social Problems. Understanding how their boys came to be who, what, and where they are is essential to the development of a decent counselor. Hard on the heels of these courses would come training in Child Guidance Through Self-Government, many of whose precepts are outlined here, and finally, Relations Counseling. In spite of a shortage of good counselors, there is a lot of fat that can be trimmed from present-day staffs, namely some of the zombies I spoke of earlier.

A lot of people become nervous when they hear the term "courses." They think of thick, unfriendly-looking books and murky language. Nonsense. All you need is the ability to read well, to comprehend what you're reading, and to express yourself in clear English (or Spanish or whatever).

Next, counselors who have been qualified must be given policy-making power in the institution through a counselor representative. This power must include the right to veto administrative proposals where they relate to working conditions. A strong counselor union is a step in the right direction. An institution runs better if working policies are arrived at through negotiation, with all concerned parties (including the boys) participating.

But most of all, the selection and development of relations counselors hinges on counselor personality, for these are the behavior models for the boys in our institutions.

"But that's imprecise," another friend objected. "There are many different kinds of personalities." I consider that to be a strength of the system, not a weakness. Look around you. Consider the guy next door, across the street, your cousin, yourself. What about them? Of whom among them could you say, "If his attitudes were adopted by an admiring antisocial youngster, the kid would be helped"? Some of them? All of them? Okay. Do all the people you have picked as good copy models have the same styles and living techniques? No, of course not. But they all, given training, would make great relations counselors because they all "have their own shit together," as the saying goes. That's what it's all about.

These boys, for whom mother is merely a prefix to an inelegant, longer word, have known that all along.